T0366828

THE

PUBLICATIONS

OF THE

Lincoln Record Society

FOUNDED IN THE YEAR

1910

VOLUME 66

FOR THE YEAR ENDING 31st AUGUST 1972

Harpswell Hall in the late Eighteenth Century. Drawing by J. C. Nattes in Lincoln Public Library

LETTERS FROM JOHN WALLACE

TO

MADAM WHICHCOT

EDITED BY

C. M. LLOYD, M.A.

AND

SOME CORRESPONDENCE OF JOHN FARDELL

DEPUTY REGISTRAR, 1802-1805

EDITED BY

MARY E. FINCH, M.A., PH.D.

PRINTED FOR

THE LINCOLN RECORD SOCIETY

BY

J. W. RUDDOCK & SONS LIMITED, LINCOLN

1973

THIS VOLUME HAS BEEN PRODUCED
WITH THE ASSISTANCE OF A GRANT FROM
THE BRITISH ACADEMY

CONTENTS

Frontispiece
HARPSWELL HALL

From the original by John Claude
Nattes in the Lincoln City Library

SOME CORRESPONDENCE
OF THE FAMILY OF
WHICHCOT OF HARPSWELL

INTRODUCTION

Among the records deposited by the trustees of the late Sir George Whichcote, Bart., of Aswarby, at the Lincolnshire Archives Office in 1952, are a large number of papers of the Whichcots of Harpswell[1] which must have come into the hands of the Aswarby branch of the family as a result of the marriage of Sir Christopher Whichcote to Jane, daughter of Thomas Whichcot of Harpswell in 1762. Thomas Whichcot died without male heir and his estates passed to his daughter at his death in 1776.

The surviving records of the Whichcots of Harpswell, apart from title deeds and estate papers, include a large number of household vouchers and many family letters. Most of the latter cover a fairly short period between about 1710 and 1730. The small group of letters printed here have been chosen for publication because of the interesting picture they give of household life and also because of the information which they contain about politics and other county affairs.

The Whichcots stemmed originally from a Shropshire family, one of whose members obtained Harpswell by marriage with Elizabeth Tyrwhitt in the mid-fifteenth century. (He was sheriff of Lincolnshire in 1466). Once settled in the county, the family proceeded to prosper and multiply. They became related by marriage in the sixteenth century to such families as the Bussys of Hougham and the Carres of Sleaford. Branches sprang up in several parts of Lincolnshire. Younger sons found their way to London and prospered in trade. It was from one of these junior branches that the baronets of Aswarby descended, obtaining their Lincolnshire seat, at Aswarby, between Sleaford and Bourne in 1723. Meanwhile the senior branch of the family remained at Harpswell.

The background necessary to follow the letters printed below begins with the career of Colonel George Whichcot, 1653-1720. He married three times: the first two wives, Frances daughter of Sir Francis Boynton of Burton Agnes, Yorks., and Isabella, widow of Darcy Stanhope of Mellwood in the Isle of Axholme need not concern us here—except to say that the Stanhope marriage was presumably the foundation for his considerable political interest in

---

[1] In the eighteenth century the Harpswell Whichcots always spelt the name without a final 'e'. The Aswarby family spelt the name 'Whichcote', certainly from the mid-eighteenth century.

Harpswell is about 12 miles N. of Lincoln, and 8 miles W. of Gainsborough.

Axholme, and also for the troublesome guardianship of his two step-grandchildren Elizabeth and Isabella Stanhope, whose upbringing, education and marriages figure prominently in his correspondence.

Our story really begins with the Colonel's return from the wars, eulogised by John Bowes, 'late Lieutenant':—

'You have been zealous for the King in Flanders
Equal to any of our Chief Commanders'.

He settled down at Harpswell, was elected M.P. for the County in 1698 and two years later married his third wife, hymned once more in the tuneful numbers of his personal Poet Laureate:—

'Poets of late to prophesy begun
Pray give me leave to prophesy a son.
A Son whose name shall fill all English ears
Both to the joy of Whichcot and of Meres'.[1]

Frances Katherine Meres was the daughter of Sir Thomas Meres and sister of Sir John Meres, who is frequently mentioned in our correspondence. This marriage brought the Colonel into relationship with a family which had considerable properties in Lincolnshire, around Kirton in Holland and at Scotton, near Gainsborough, also in Leicestershire, where Sir John Meres' principal seat was Kirby Bellars, and in London where Sir John dabbled in high finance, speculative building and other enterprises.

The marriage was followed by a trip to London where many new household furnishings for Harpswell were purchased; the old silver plate and pewter were exchanged for new: beds, a cradle and quilts were bought. Then the Colonel and his bride returned to Harpswell where they produced in the next six years, two sons, Thomas and John, and two daughters, Katherine and Elizabeth.

The Colonel's surviving correspondence down to his death in 1720 relates principally to the upbringing of his family and his Stanhope wards. The boys apparently attended school in Brigg (John certainly did) and later went on to Cambridge. Both his own daughters, and Isabella and Elizabeth Stanhope, went to school in London, to Mrs. Dorothy Draper in Park Street, Westminster. Their letters home are full of interest for the light they throw both on their own education and on the busy London scene at the end of Queen Anne's reign and accession of George I.

They saw the Queen's body carried to the painted chamber at Westminster:—

"and there were two trumpets that played very dismally and the horses that carried the hearse wore black cloths".[2]

They watched the entrance of George I into the capital from their balcony in the company of Richard Steele, very ill with gout and lifted in and out of the room by two porters, and mightily pleased

[1] L.A.O. Anderson 5/1/18.
[2] L.A.O. Aswarby (hereafter referred to as "Asw."), 10/18/2.

with the company of Miss Whichcot and the younger Miss Stanhope.[1]
All the girls wore ribbons lettered in gold:—

"Let us with joy King George receive
Who only can our loss relieve".

More equivocal were the verses scribbled on a wall in St. Paul's
churchyard:—

"Brandy face Anne is now in her tomb
And George, a cuckold, is come in her room".[2]

Jacobite agents were trying to stir up trouble, and politics caused
ill-feeling even within the walls of Mrs. Draper's establishment; for
that lady lost several pupils by her loyalty, and could not but regret
that "to be an honest well-wisher to the Government raises one such
enemies".

When the Colonel died in 1720 his son Thomas was at Magdalene,
John was at school, and both the girls were approaching marriage-
able age. Great economies were needed, for the estate was not a large
one, consisting of little more than the parish of Harpswell, with a
rental of only about £1500 a year. Many of the household goods were
sold and Mrs. Whichcot, after hesitating some time over the problem
of whether or not to stay at home (she even seems for a while to
have considered renting the house), went on her travels, lodging for
a long period in London, later at Rackheath near Norwich with her
sister and brother-in-law, Sir Horatio and Lady Pettus. Harpswell
was not, in fact, leased, because then there might have been no house
available for the eldest son when he decided to marry and settle
down.

Thomas Whichcot's future was the first priority. After finishing
his education at Cambridge he was entered at Gray's Inn. Sir John
Meres was urgent for business, writing to his nephew:—

"Although old Dickenson [one of the Harpswell farmers] says
he would rather see half a score fat bullocks in a field, I thought
it had not been quite so with you".[3]

In the end, however, Thomas was to become what Sir John described
rather patronisingly as a:—

"Country gentleman, managing and taking care of his own,
rather than one that shall pursue any difficult study to attain
honour or profit".[4]

(At least, Whichcot did not plunge into a career of high, or low,
finance as his uncle would, perhaps, have liked; he did, of course,
serve for 34 years from 1740 to 1774 as M.P. for Lincolnshire.)

The second child, and eldest daughter, Katherine, was fairly
soon settled to the satisfaction of her mother and elder brother.
She married John Maddison of Ketton, Rutland, in 1723, and references to occasional visits to Ketton and the speedy increase of the
Maddison family are found fairly frequently in the letters printed

[1] Asw. 10/19/2.
[2] Asw. 10/18/11.
[3] Asw. 2/114/5.
[4] Asw. 10/26/20.

below. Equally frequent references occur (often in far from enthusiastic terms) to the two younger children, John and Elizabeth ("Mrs. Betty"). John followed his brother to Cambridge, was ordained priest in 1729 and, in the following year, both he and Elizabeth married, in neither case with the approval of their relatives. Sir John Meres however consoled Mrs. Whichcot with the reflection that it must be a relief to have all her children settled and that in the younger children's eagerness for marriage they were but following the example of their father, "he being much addicted to Matrimony".[1]

So much for the general family background, but a few further explanatory notes seem necessary for an understanding of the letters, other than what can be explained briefly in footnotes.

It is important to understand the vital position of Sir John Meres in the Whichcot family's plans and ambitions. He was rich, he was eccentric, he was unmarried; Mrs. Whichcot was one of several sisters (Lady Pettus was another; Mrs. Hayley, wife of the Dean of Chichester was another). There was hope that the Whichcot children might be assisted by Sir John's wealth and influence during his lifetime and obtain a good share in his will, but not if they offended him. In 1720 Colonel Whichcot was angry with Thomas at Cambridge for associating with those "who are not in your Uncle's interest. Your Uncle may be your friend".[2] After Colonel Whichcot's death Sir John seems, on the whole, to have stood by the bereaved family (though a refusal, on the grounds of poverty, to lend £100 to Mrs. Whichcot was not an auspicious beginning).[3] He gave an allowance to John Whichcot while he was at Cambridge. Thomas Whichcot was ultimately to receive a large increase of estate and fortune at his uncle's death, but in the meanwhile tact was needed to keep Sir John in a good humour and he had to be consulted on matters such as Thomas's proposed marriage. This position of Meres as the fountain head from which wealth might flow to, or be withheld from the Whichcot family, explains several references in John Wallace's letters to Mrs. Whichcot, as where he says that Mrs. Betty will make a fine young lady and please Sir John (8), and his carefulness to explain to her that he canvassed the Meres tenants for Mr. Viner at Sir John's own express command (14).

Of John Wallace himself, the writer of the letters, we know little beyond what can be learned from his own correspondence, and the entry of his burial in 1736 in the Harpswell parish register. He was obviously employed by Colonel Whichcot in some capacity as early as 1713, when we have a letter from him to one of the Colonel's creditors about how money will be paid.[4] After the Colonel's death he seems to have remained at Harpswell as steward, in charge of the estates and household during the absences of Thomas Whichcot and

[1] Asw. 10/28/18. [2] Asw. 2/116/9.
[3] Asw. 10/26/33. [4] Asw. 2/97/11.

his mother. At one time, when Mrs. Whichcot was partly resolved to stay on at Harpswell, there was talk of his only coming over from Lincoln every now and again. But, in the event, he appears to have stayed there pretty well permanently, looking after both Thomas Whichcot's affairs (whom he calls usually "My Master") and also those of Mrs. Whichcot.

A vivid picture of an empty house with its owners absent emerges from his earlier letters. A fire grate had to be borrowed when the Maddisons stayed (15). Most of the mice were "destroyed with wire mouse-trapps and famine" (7). But, however bare of furnishings the Hall was, it was kept in repair and outside in the Park improvements were in progress. Fish ponds were being scoured out and restocked and trees planted (e.g., 7, 11, 21).

Many of Wallace's letters to Mrs. Whichcot either accompany money, or advise her on when and how she will receive the next remittance, to pay for her board and lodging, teas, wine, and other necessaries. These remittances were delayed at times by difficulties in getting in the rents when times were bad for the farmers, as in February 1726 when there was a bad outbreak of sheep rot (28). In 1723 also there had been complaints of the badness of the times, when the season was so late that young apples hung on the trees as big as nutmegs in late November (8).

Sometimes the vagaries of the post made correspondence difficult. Letters from Norwich normally arrived on the fifth day (28), but bad weather could have a disastrous effect: on Jan. 12th 1726 the Post Boy had not been to Harpswell since the New Year owing to the frost and snow (25).

Apart from his duties at Harpswell John Wallace seems also to have been regarded as a suitable person to canvass the tenants at election time in favour of the Whichcots' political friends. Early in 1723 he accompanied the Whig candidate, Mr. Viner, into the Isle of Axholme (12). "My Master's Interest and Creditt engages me to go about this County to serve Mr. Viner", he says, before departing to canvass the Meres tenants in the parts of Holland (13). (Shortly after Colonel Whichcot's death, Sir John Meres had suggested that it was as well to keep up his political interests if this were not too expensive, and this advice seems to have been followed.)[1] At Gainsborough the Tory mob pelted Mr. Viner and his friends with dirt, but he reports triumphantly later, were likely to suffer for their insolence by having a troop of soldiers quartered on them (12), (15).

Madam Whichcot seems to have relied on John Wallace, as much as anything else, for gossip from "happy Harpswell", a place which all the Whichcots loved and longed to return to. In this respect, although he was continually apologising for the shortage of news, she cannot have been disappointed. Apart from the constant details of events at Harpswell itself; births, marriages and deaths among

[1] Asw. 10/28/2.

the servants and tenants; there is much information on the Whichcots' neighbours, particularly their nearest and greatest neighbours,
the Saundersons of Glentworth.

The 6th Viscount Castleton died in 1723, leaving Glentworth to
his distant maternal relative, Colonel Thomas Lumley, who took the
additional surname of Saunderson, and was to succeed his brother
in 1740 as 4th Earl of Scarbrough. The Saundersons provided matter
for John Wallace to write about, both as friends of the Whichcots,
as possible sources of advancement for his master (there was a
suggestion that Thomas Whichcot should accompany Col. Saunderson on his embassy to Portugal, when Wallace hoped "you'll have
the pleasure of seeing him make his fortune" (7)), but also, above all,
as strange and wonderful animals whose style of living was at
complete variance with the frugality of Harpswell, and brought a
breath of the great world to the neighbourhood. The prodigality
of the Glentworth family obviously amazed him ("Seventy stone of
beefe and about Two Quarters of Wheat is their Weekly stint").
Tolerant amazement was apt to give way to annoyance, however,
when he found that this plenteous living was pushing up the price
of butter in Gainsborough market to 7d. a pound (25). A great event
in the neighbourhood was the entertainment by Sir Thomas Saunderson of "the Body of the city of Lincoln", who went away crying,
'A Saunderson! A Saunderson! ' when he promised them a pair of
iron gates and pillars of stone from Roche Abbey for their new
church (26).

But acceptable as such titbits of local gossip were, Mrs. Whichcot
probably found most acceptable the news of her own family, particularly of Thomas. (Perhaps news of John complaining of poverty
and demanding money was not so welcome (19)). John Wallace,
whatever his position was officially called, was obviously on intimate terms with the family, and there were few if any secrets
from him. From the whole series of letters a fascinating picture can
be formed of the younger bachelor squire, serious but not solemn,
fully aware of his financial position and the need for economy and
the careful choice of a wife, conscientiously beginning at the age of 23
to take upon himself those public duties which were necessary to his
'interest and credit': trustee of Kirton in Lindsey Free School (4),
Commissioner of Sewers (32). Mrs. Whichcot was doubtless pleased
to know that her son had enjoyed good health and brisk hunting all
winter and to hear his usual *modus vivendi* (11) and that the Harpswell housekeeping coped with visits such as the Saundersons and
their friends, who, coming out of curiosity to see how Thomas lived
and 'to laugh at his housekeeping', went away very pleased with
their entertainment (26).

The combination of Wallace's letters and those of Thomas Whichcot himself give a lively account of the latter's cautious courtship
in 1725-6 of a lady who is never specifically named. She may have

been a Chaplin of Tathwell (23) or possibly a Tyrwhitt: a rumour
of his courtship of a member of this family had been heard by Sir
John Meres in 1723.[1] Whoever she was, Wallace was pleased to
observe that 'Love's greatest efforts can't taint his reason'. One of
his first steps was to sound out Sir John's attitude (21). Soon there
was a rumour among Meres' Scotton tenants that the estate had
now been given to Thomas Whichcot who was about to marry (22).
But this matrimonial campaign came to nothing. In December 1725
he set out for Louth Assembly, determined to be satisfied one way
or another (23) but the result must have been communicated to
Mrs. Whichcot by word of mouth. In fact he did not marry until
1729, when his bride was Eliza Maria, daughter of Francis Anderson
of Manby.

　　With the return of Mrs. Whichcot to Harpswell in 1727, Wallace's
letters cease, although he lived for another nine years (apparently
at Harpswell where he was buried on 12th April 1736, outliving his
mistress by three years). From other correspondents we can learn
something of the family's history during those years but none of
them, naturally enough, retail the gossip of the neighbourhood so
conscientiously and so entertainingly as he did.

[1] Asw. 10/28/5.

1. *[Address torn off]*   [? 1721 or 1722][1]
Honoured Madam,
   My Master was the other night with Sir John Meres, who desires
that you will send him up some wild fowl and a Hare, if they can be
gott. My Master[2] and my selfe was to have left London as Yesterday,
but Lord Castleton[3] stops my Master by engaging him to goe with
his Lordship to the Lincolnshire Club which is to be at Pontack's
next Munday, where a great many Persons of Quality will meet, to
whom my Lord will Introduce him, and the next day wee are to sett
out for Cambridge.[4] I shall forbear Madam to give you any further
account of our proceedings here, because in a little time I hope to
have an opportunity of delivering itt more perfectly to you, than a
blundring Pen can Relate. I Presume Madam you have no further
business here, then what I had your directions for when att Harpswell, because I have not received any Commands from you since I
came hither. My Master Presents his Duty to your selfe and his love
to Mrs. Kath[5] and Miss Bett,[6] which concludes this trouble.
[Asw. 10/24/1]   from
                                  Your Most obedient Humble
                                       Servant,
                                            J. Wallace

   [1] This must be earlier than May 1723 when Lord Castleton died and probably dates
from 1721 or 1722.
   [2] Thomas Whichcot (1700-76), the elder son, is referred to throughout these
letters as "my Master".
   [3] James Saunderson, 1st Earl of Castleton. He died 23rd May 1723.
   [4] Thomas Whichcot was at Magdalene College from 1719, probably to 1722.
   [5] Katherine Whichcot (1701-87), elder daughter. She married John Maddison
(1691-1746) of Ketton, Rutland, and Stainton le Vale on July 9th 1723. She is
referred to in all the following letters as Mrs. Maddison.
   [6] Elizabeth Whichcot (1706-74). She married William Bassett (1703-65) on 19th
Feb. 1730. (cf. no. 16 n. 2).

2. *To Madam Whichcot to be left at Mrs. Draper's[1] in Park Street in
   Westminster.*
                                       Harpswell, Sept. 2nd 1723
   I hope before this comes to your hand, you'll be recovered of the
Fateague and disorder that your Journey occationed and setled in
such lodgings as you like, which I shall be mighty glad to hear.
   Wee got very well to Harpswell, without the least Accident, of
Saturday night, and this day I have turned your Coach mares to
Grass, and shall make it my business to dispose of a Pair of them, as
soon as I can meet with a Chapman.
   When the Races[2] are over I will give you a letter of all the News
I hear, in the mean time begg leave to conclude.
[P.S.] As Lord Castleton's Old Coachman Daniel was driving Mr.
Saunderson[3] betwixt Northallerton and Durham, he fell off the

Coach box, and broak his legg, which in three or four days killed him.

[Asw. 10/27/1]

[1] Dorothy Draper kept a school, which had earlier been attended by the Whichcot girls.

[2] For information on Lincoln races, a great social magnet in the eighteenth century, see Sir Francis Hill, *Georgian Lincoln*, p. 16, Cambridge University Press, 1966.

[3] Presumably Thomas Lumley (c. 1691-1752) who took the additional surname of Saunderson on the death of his cousin, Lord Castleton, to whose estates he succeeded. Succeeded his brother as third Earl of Scarbrough, 1740.

3. *To Madam Whichcot at Mrs. Fashion's*[1] *over-against the King's Arms in Little Queen Street in Westminster.*

Humbly Present.

Harpswell, Sept. 8th 1723

Honoured Madam,

I am very glad to hear by your letter that you got well to London and hope this will find you in a setled state of good health, and determined to continue in the Lodgings you say you like without differing about the Price.

I have sent the Box with the directions you ordered and desire that Ned may be sent for it next Saturday, to the Red-lyon in Aldersgate Street, and ask the Carrier or the Book keeper for the Key that belongs it, which I have also sent up. I hope everything that's in it will get safe to you and, if I have not put all up, it is because the Box is so weak it would not hold more. The Carriage is paid. I have no other news Madam from the Races, than that there was a great Assembly of Quality and Gentry at Lincoln, amongst which was the Duke of Rutland,[2] the Duke of Ancaster,[3] Earl of Hallifax,[4] Lord Tyrconel,[5] Sir Marmeduke Wivill,[6] etc. His Grace of Rutland was Mrs. Maddison's Partner, but who my Master danced with, I supose he'll give you an Account himselfe with several Particulars that I know not. I heartily wish Miss Betty a Pleasant Journey with her Spark. And am . . . .

[P.S.] I humbly begg Madam that you'll be pleased to tell Betty,[7] that her Mantua and Pettycoat, her Stays and Cloak shall come together the journey after this, if she sends no word to the Contrary. Mr. Saunderson is to be at Glentworth[8] of Wednesday or Thursday next, but how long his stay will be is not known.

In my next Madam I hope I shall have more news to tell you.

[Asw. 10/27/2]

[1] There is a receipted account from Avis Fashion for £32 for Mrs. Whichcot's lodging, at £1 per week, from 2nd Sept. 1723 to 12th Apr. 1724. (Asw. 10/32/3).

[2] John Manners (1696-1779), 3rd Duke of Rutland. Although the main seat was at Belvoir Castle, just over the Leicestershire border, the family had extensive estates in Lincolnshire.

[3] Peregrine Bertie (1686-1742), 2nd Duke of Ancaster. Succeeded his father in July 1723.

[4] George Montague (c. 1685-1739), 4th Earl of Halifax. He married Mary, daughter of the 1st Earl of Scarbrough.

[5] John Brownlow (1690-1754), son and heir of Sir John Brownlow, 4th Bart. Created Viscount Tyrconnel in 1718. M.P. Grantham, 1713-5, 1722-41; Lincolnshire 1715-22. A letter survives from him to Mrs. Whichcot in 1721, after Colonel Whichcot's death, soliciting the Whichcot political interest, (Asw. 10/35/4).

[6] Sir Marmaduke Wyvill (1690-1754), 6th Bart., 1690-1754, of Constable Burton, Yorks.

[7] Betty Beckerin[g], apparently Mrs. Whichcot's maid, cf. no. 8.

[8] Glentworth Hall, formerly the seat of the Wrays, had now passed to the Saundersons. The parish bounds Harpswell on the South.

4.   [Sept. 18th 1723]

My Master is now at Harpswell where he received a letter by the last Post from you, which was very welcome to me, the account it gave of your Receiving the box, which I hope was to your satisfaction. Colonel Saunderson,[1] being now at Glentworth, engages my Master there every day, but he stays there only a Fortnight and then returns to London, and from thence to Portugal[2] after Christmas. The Colonel is (as I hear by the by) very well assured that Sir C. W.[3] can't get the Estate he aims at, which is Occationed by a deed not being Rightly Executed, for, Instead of three Witnesses to it, there are only two which makes it Invalid. This I had from my Master and I suppose it is at Present a Secret.

The Day after Michaelmas day you'll Receive of William Dickinson[4] at your own Lodgings fifty Pounds, and when I have another opportunity shall order you more, but as yet I have received very little of those Rents that are due. I shall send Mrs. Cox's Clothes to Ketton next Monday.

My Master is going this day to meet Sir William Monson,[5] Mr. Anderson[6] etc. at Kerton, to be made one of the Trustees for that Free School,[7] and at Night is to have the Honour of Colonel Saunderson's Company to drink his health, this being the 18th day of Sept. 1723.

I am at a very great loss Madam for News to fill this Paper, the Country has so little in it, and Indeed was it not for the Middle Paragraph, it would be very dear at the price.

[P.S.] I need only write Harpswell because you have the date above. My Mother[8] Presentes her most Humble Service to you, and Miss Betty.

[Endorsed] J. W. about money. £50.
[Asw. 10/27/3]

[1] He had been appointed Lieut. Col. of Lord Hinchinbroke's Regiment of Foot in 1717. Wallace must have learned his correct title only on his arrival at Glentworth.

[2] Colonel Saunderson was Envoy Extraordinary, later Plenipotentiary, to Portugal from 1722 to 1725. He came home on leave from June 1723 to September 1724 (Horn, *British Diplomatic Representatives*, 1689-1789, Camden Third Series, 46, 1932).

[3] Perhaps Sir Cecil Wray (cf. no. 8 n. 3) hoped to succeed to some of the old Wray estates on the death of Lord Castleton.

B

[4] Dickinson was, and is, a very common name in this part of Lincolnshire. A William Dickinson of Harpswell, yeoman, died in 1729 (L.A.O. Stow Wills 1728-31/61). Among several sons was another William, who may well be the man mentioned here. (Cf. no. 6. n. 1).
[5] Sir William Monson (d. 1727), 4th Bart. of Burton by Lincoln.
[6] Francis Anderson of Manby (1675-1747), later to become Thomas Whichcot's father-in-law.
[7] In 1764 Thomas Whichcot was the sole surviving trustee for the free grammar school of Kirton in Lindsey (*Charity Commissioners Report:* Lincs., 1819-37, p. 453).
[8] When Wallace died in 1736, administration of his goods was granted to his mother, Mary Wallace of Lincoln, widow. (L.A.O. Stow Admons. 1721-40/397).

Harpswell, Sept. 25th 1723
5.

By the last Post the Enclosed came to my hands which I have sent to you by this first opportunity, not knowing but it may be of consequence.

My Master has a desire to fence off a Piece of Ground in the Upper Park for a Paddock, which he will do at his own charge with Stoops & Rales; it is the farthest corner of the Upper Park next Harry's Lane. If you please to give your consent to the doing of it, he'll Pay you what Rent you'll desire; the compass of Ground is only two Acres and a halfe. This affair, Madam, Requires your speedy Answer, for without such fine Weather he can't get his Fencing from the Wood. I can only say it won't be much damage to the Park and it is the worst Piece of Ground in it, and the Partition may be Removed at Pleasure.
[Asw. 10/27/4]

Harpswell, Oct. 5th 1723
6.

Mrs. Dickenson Received three Keys by her son[1] last Thursday, with a very strict charge, and of Fryday morning she came and see the Plate taken out, the Keys Sealed and all put into the Box, which was accordingly nailed up in her presence. This Proceeding Madam I hope will give you satisfaction.

There are ten Huccaback Napkins, one Huccaback Towell and a Damask Table Cloth sent; if you thought of a Huccaback Table Cloth there was only two made for the long Table in the Glass Parlour and Mrs. Dickinson thought you could not want one of that Shape, so she did not send it. Mrs. Betty's hat and Betty Beckerin's Clothes are also sent, all which I hope you'll receive next Saturday by the Lincoln Carriage.

The Ewes in the Park being fit to kill, I have sold them to the Butcher, and (with William Dickinson's advise) shall put a little money to the Ewes price, and buy fifteen or sixteen lean Ewes, to bring Lambs against you come hom in the Spring, or to make Money of them as you please. One of the Coach Mares my Master has taken, and the other that is to be sold, will give a very little Money, she being blind.

My Master has quite laid aside the thoughts of making a Paddock, and therefore the Parks will remain as they are.

My Ignorance Madam of Publick Funds, makes me Incapable of giving any Answer to that part of your letter. Mr. Bradshaw has promised to come, and give the Gardener his Opinion about cutting the Trees in the Park, which, when he has done, I will let you know what he advises.

Last Saturday Patty was brought to Bed of a Boy, and does very well, and about Wednesday last Mrs. Harvey was brought to Bed of a Son and is in a Good way of Recovery.

Colonel Saunderson leaves Glentworth next Thursday, and of Fryday, his Honour and my Master dines at Ketton, which I have let Mr. Maddison know by this Post. As soon as the Colonel comes to London he Intends to waite of you, which is all at Present.

[P.S.] William Dickinson and his wife returns you thanks for your Favours to their two sons.

My Master gives his Duty to You, he is with the Colonel at Glentworth every day till Bed time.

[Asw. 10/27/5]

¹ Mrs. Dickinson may be the wife of William Dickinson, senior, mentioned in no. 4 n. 4; in that case her son will be William Dickinson, junior.

Harpswell, Oct 23rd 1723

7.

Last Night by the Markett People from Gainsbrough I received the Honour of Yours, and am very glad you are Recovered of your disorder and that the Box came safe to your hands.

My Master has been from Harpswell this fortnight, but now I expect him (according to his own promise) every day. He has promissed Colonel Saunderson to go with him to Lisbon in February, in the mean time the Colonel has Invited him to his house in Arlington Street, and Assures him his Expences every where with the Colonel shall be very small. The Colonel's favour and the Opportunity of this Journey will doubtless be of great advantage to my Master and I hope you'll have the Pleasure of seeing him make his Fortune.

I am very sorry Miss Betty's stay at Tunbridge is so long; I doubt she'll have much ado to make that Improvement she might have done had she stay'd with you, and I am very sencible she has cost you a great deal of Money in Equiping for that Journey. She ought at her return to be very Dutyful to so Indulgent a Parent and Indeed I not only hope, but believe, she will.

I will take all the Care I can to put George Dickinson¹ in a Method to Remind Sir John of his Godson,² and Intend to meet George next Tuesday at Gainsborough upon no other business which I hope will be attended with good success.

I have got the brewhouse Pond Cleaned, which was very necessary; the Expence only 2s. 4d., and in the Upper Park Pond I put in last Munday, one hundred and twenty-seven Brace of young Carp, which I got of Mr. Bussey to try our Pond with. If they do well they will Stock other Ponds. Richard[3] has got seeds of Ash, Lime, Thorn and a Peck of Holly berries out of Yorkshire, in order to Improve the Nursery, which place Colonel Saunderson see and mightily liked, and advised to stub up all the old Apple trees to enlarge the Nursery, which (when you have Concidered) if you give orders shall be carefully done.

John Green is now making two doors for the Orchard Seat, and of Munday Dick Middleton comes to point the Windows, and mend the Tiling where it wants.[4] The Park shall be hill'd[5] when the season serves, but at Present the Ground is too hard for that work. I take care to see the Furniture opened and shaked, once in a week or ten days, and as yet there is no damage happened to any of it; and now I hope there won't, for wee have destroyed most of the Mise with wire Mouse trapps and Famine, our housekeeping not affording anything for Vermin. I have sold the Blind Mare to Joseph Dickinson[6] for five pounds ten shillings. He will be in London in a fortnight and then will pay you for the mare, and his halfe years Rent also, which is twelve pound ten shillings so that he will pay you in all eighteen Pounds, and then you must give him a shilling for luck of the Mare, as the custom is amongst Jockeys.

Your affairs here Madam shall be carefully looked after and your Commands that I shall at any time Receive be strictly obeyed. [P.S.] I will talk with my Master when he comes about the Certainty of his Allowance to his Brother and Sister. My Mother Presentes her most Humble Service to you. [Asw. 10/27/6]

¹ Probably another son of William Dickinson, senior (no. 4 n. 1), whose will mentions a son George, and apparently steward of the Meres estates in the area.

² Sir John Meres (d. 1736). Mrs. Whichcot's brother. His godson was her younger son, John (1702-50).

³ There is a voucher for payment to Richard Stones for vegetable seeds in 1722-3, (Asw. 2/100/16; 60).

⁴ John Green, for labour, and Richard Middleton, for tiling roof and mending walls, both appear in the vouchers for 1722-3 (Asw. 2/100/13; 62).

⁵ Definitely 'h', not 't.' Possibly refers to ridging up the land for drainage purposes.

⁶ Possibly another son of William Dickinson senior, but no Joseph is mentioned in his will (cf. no. 4 n. 4).

Harpswell, November 2nd 1723

8.

I am very glad Mrs. Betty is got well to you and don't doubt but, with the assistance of Mr. Groscot, she'll make a very fine young lady and please Sir John so well as to Engage his Favour and affection. I went last Tuesday to meet George Dickinson at Gainsborough and talked with him about Mr. John's affair and told him the great difference there was in the Expenses, betwixt his school learning and his University Education. George seem'd to Understand very well what I told him and said that at Christmas, when he made up his Accounts, he would speak to Sir John and Press him to Enlarge his Old Allowances as far as he dare venture, and will then waite of you and Acquaint you with the Answer he receives.

To Encourage the Carp by Conveying Fresh Water to them makes it necessary to Clear the Ditch also, which I will get done in a little time, and will also begin to stub the apple trees, as soon as I receive your Commands. As to the Expence, the Trees will pay it, and as to a place for a New Orchard, the Enlarging the Kitchen Garden to the Hollow Way in the Park is certainly the Propperest of any Place about the Homestead.

I was Extreamly sorry when I heard the Melancholy News of Mr. Pettus's Death, Mr. John Pettus[1] was here but my Master and I was out and did not see him. He stayed about two hours and dined with my Mother, of Mutton and Rabbitts, and seemed (she said) very well pleased with his Baite.

I believe Madam you and Sir John both will receive Letters from my Master this Post, who is now at Harpswell, and (Thank God) in very Good Health.

I was very Glad of the opportunity of sending that small sum by Joseph Dickinson, which I hope he'll have paid before this comes to you. There is a very great Complaint in the Country of the badness of the Times, which Effects every body's Tenants and Consequently yours amongst the Rest, that as yet I have not Received Twelve Pounds in Rent, but as soon as Martinmas is turned I hope to have it come in.

You are very kind Madam in giving Betty Beckerin the liberty to see the fine Sights of the Town, and I am very glad she is pleased with them.

The Weather till this Moment has been very Dry, but now it has begun to Rain. I hope it will Continue a Many Days.
[P.S.] I don't hear of Sir Cecil's[2] leaving the country as yet; but am Informed Sir John Tyrwhitt[3] will not be in Town till after Christmas. My Master gives his Duty to You and will write to You next Post. He is tired with writing to Sir John.
[Asw. 10/27/7]

[1] Sir Horatio Pettus (d. 1731), 4th Bart. of Rackheath, Norfolk, married Elizabeth Meres, Mrs. Whichcot's sister. Their eldest son Thomas died in 1723; his brother John (d. 1743), succeeded him as heir and was ultimately the 5th Baronet.
[2] Presumably Sir Cecil Wray (d. 1736), 11th Bart, "of Glentworth", but now living at Branston, near Lincoln.
[3] Sir John Tyrwhitt (d. 1741), 5th Bart. of Stainfield. M.P. for the City of Lincoln, 1715-34.

[Nov. 22nd 1723]

9.

I have not Received a letter from you in answer to my last, but the distance of time betwixt my last letter and this makes it my Duty to give you some account of your affairs here. The Account Madam betwixt my Master and you (when you left Harpswell) was, that he then owed you fifty-one Pounds sixteen shillings, Twenty Pounds of which he paid you at Ketton. The remainder which is £31 16s. is still Indebted to you, besides what is due to you since then for Mr. John and Mrs. Betty, which I suppose he'll pay to your Satisfaction, but wee shall not settle the Accounts till next Munday, he being now at Mr. Pelham's¹ therefore I can't as yet be more Particular in this affair. I have got the Ditch Scowered very well and it has made a very good Currant for the Water, which till now has been Extremely scarce. The Labourers (viz.) John Abraham, John Housham and Edward Watson (the latter having been once asked in the Church with a servant of Thomas Codd's² of Hemswell) begins to-Morrow to Stub the Apple trees in the Orchard, which will be done with a very little money out of Pockett. I have got Two doors made for the Orchard Seat and Primed them. The Hilling³ the Park and leading Rubbish can't be performed as yet. When I go to Lincoln I'll be sure to Pay Mrs. Mackinder.⁴ Sir John Madam was very Kind in his Present of Venison to you, but much more so in the Message that attended it. He seldome declares his thoughts by words and you are the most Capable of any Person to Understand what he means by his hints:

When you are tired with London, (which I hope won't be long ere you are), I humbly begg leave to wish you a Good Journey to Harpswell Rather than to Norfolke and don't doubt but you'll find every thing to your satisfaction here.

[P.S.] We have in our Neighbourhood, Occationed by the Wanness of the Season, Fruit heer in Blossom, Young Apples as bigg as Nutmeggs, and Young Crows in Several Places, but in our own Garden I can't see any Flowers, or fruit.

Mr. Crow of Spridlington⁵ is lately Dead and Mr. Jolland⁶ went with Mr. Scrop's⁷ letter, and my Master's to waite on Sir Bryan Broughton⁸ for the living of Aisthorpe worth £441 a Year paid in Money, which Sir Bryan gave him at the very first word.

I humbly begg Pardon for the Extraordinary expence of this, and that you'll be pleased to give Ned leave to carry it to Mr. Vaux who he will find at the Exchequer office in the Temple or at his House in White Lyon Court in Fleet Street.

[Endorsed Nov. 22nd.]

[Asw. 10/27/8]

¹ Probably Charles Pelham of Brocklesby, c. 1679-1763.
² Codds were as numerous as Dickinsons in the area, especially in Hemswell, the parish immediately North of Harpswell.

[3] Cf. no. 7 n. 5.
[4] Mrs. Mackinder received payment for biscuits and cakes in 1722-3 (Asw. 2/100/32).
[5] Thomas Crow had held the living of Aisthorpe, about seven miles South of Harpswell, since 1674, and that of Spridlington, about the same distance South East, since 1671.
[6] William Jolland, a college contemporary of Thomas Whichcot, was vicar of Aisthorpe and Grayingham from 1724 until his death in 1733.
[7] Gervase Scrope of Cockerington, 1682-1741.
[8] Sir Brian Broughton (d. 1724), 3rd Bart. of Broughton, Staffs. His mother was Rhoda, daughter of John Amcotts, of Aisthorpe.

[Dec. 7th 1723]

10.
   I Humbly Begg leave (in answer to the first line of your letter) to assure you that I was not guilty of any failure of Memory; for your letter by Joseph Dickinson bore date two days before mine was wrote, and therefore could not be in Answer to my last but one. This charge I thought Necessary to clear my selfe of, because a Shortness of Memory is (I think) only a more favourable phrase for Neglect of Duty, which I hope I shall never be guilty of.
   My Master leaves Harpswell next Tuesday and intends in a few days to be at Cambridge. I have given him twenty pounds, fourteen shillings and ten pence to Pay Mr. John's Quarterage and, there being another due in about a fortnight, I have also Paid to my Master to carry to the Tutor, fifteen guineas towards the Christmas Quarterage which I believe will very near clear it. Munday sen-night Mr. Hudson will pay you on Mr. Dickinson's Account thirty pounds, and what more you want be pleased give me notice, that I may take care to send it as Conveniently as I can. My Master leaves a pretty deal of Rents behind him, and has given me orders to Pay you all your Money as soon as I receive them, an account of which I have set down in the Postscript.
   If Mr. Maddison and his Lady comes to Harpswell I will do all that is in my Power to make things Convenient for them, but there is no Grates out for the Chambers, nor more than two Dozen of Plates. Their Linnen etc. they must bring with them, but I have not heard any thing from them so believe they won't come.
   I am very well satisfied, Madam, that every Penny which will be laid out (for it can't be called Spent) in Mrs. Betty Whichcot's Education will be Strictly answered in a Fine Accomplished Young Lady, for no Person can be more Capable of Improvement than her selfe, and such a Capacity attended with an Ambitious desire to Excell must make her very Compleat. Sir William Massingberd[1] (wee hear) is Dead, but who puts up for the County is not yet known. The Poor shall be served as usual, and every other Command from you shall always be readily Obeyed.

	£	s.	d.
[On Dorse] A Quarter's board for Mr. John, Mrs. Katherine and Mrs. Betty, due 7th June, 1723	25	0	0
Halfe a year board for Mr. John and Miss Betty due 7th Dec. 1723	25	0	0
Board due for my Master for himselfe and two servants	26	16	0
Due to you in all	76	16	0
Paid to you at Ketton in Part	20	0	0
Remains due to you which I am to Pay	56	16	0

[Endorsed] J. W. about Money December 7th. 1723.
[Asw. 10/27/9]

---

[1] Sir William Massingberd (1677-1723), 3rd Bart. of Gunby. M.P. for Lincolnshire, 1720-23.

Harpswell, Dec. 23rd 1723

11.

Though I had no Commands from you to send anything to London, I have ventured to Pack up in a Basket a Goose, a Young Turkey Cock and a Hare, which if they come safe to your hands I shall be very glad. Be pleased to send next Saturday to the Carrier's Inn for them. If You like what I have done in this, You may order a Hare and some more Turkeys, with Betty Beckerin's Directions how to put them up, and I will be sure to send them. I write this day that you may send your orders to me against Saturday, and I will send to Gainsbrough on purpose for the letter.

I have got about halfe the New Work in the Nursery turned over and Planted with Ash, Oak and Dutch Elms, and in a fortnight more the whole will be finished, and when you see it I am sure you'll be Extreamly pleased. The Park shall be Hilled[1] and the Rubbish led into it, when this work is over.

I presume by this time you have seen my Master who left Lincoln last Fryday Seven-night in very good health. I find you have received the thirty pounds I mentioned in my last, and when you want more Money be pleased to give me timely Notice for Money is hard to get.

[P.S.] I begg leave to wish you and Mrs. Betty a Merry Christmas and Many Happy Years.

Our Christmas here is likely to be very Melancholy for want of Your Presence. The Poor returns their Humble thanks.

[Endorsed] Dec. 23rd. Money £30.
[Asw. 10/27/10]

---

[1] Cf. no. 6 n. 5.

[? Jan. 1724]

12.

I was last Fryday at Lincoln Soliciting some Freeholders in favour of Mr. Viner[1] and there happened to meet with Mr. Viner himselfe who sent to speak with me, and desired I would go with him into the Isle,[2] which I did accordingly and have been there ever since Sunday last. Mr. Viner came to Epworth of Munday accompanied by Mr. Scrope, Mr. Anderson, Mr. Boucherett,[3] Mr. Healey[4] and Mr. Dempster.[5] They have got the Freeholders entire in Epworth, Belton, Crowle, Luddington and Althorpe but as to Haxey and Owston there are several Engaged for Sir Nevil,[6] but the Gentlemen are going this day to every Freeholder's house in these two Parishes and does not doubt but to re-gain most of them that have already Promissed. The Gentleman that has made this Interest for Sir Nevil is Mr. Hoole,[7] the Minister of Haxey, who was bred a[? Presidential],[8] and was the last Election a very great Friend to Mr. Bertie;[9] but this County very much abounds with such Reverend Gentlemen. I must attend Mr. Viner till he leaves the Isle which will be to Morrow and then I shall return to my duty at Harpswel. I am just going to take Horse and have only time to Acquaint you that there will be a Brace of Hares at the Carrier's next Saturday directed for you, and begg leave to Conclude.

[P.S.] Mr. Viner, Mr. Pelham, Mr. Scrope and Mr. Boucherett was last Saturday Mobbed in Gainsborough Streets and dirt thrown at them in a Shameful Manner.

[Asw. 10/27/11]

1 Robert Vyner (c. 1685-1777), of Gautby. M.P. for Lincolnshire, 1724-61.
2 Isle of Axholme.
3 Matthew Boucherett of North Willingham and Stallingbrough, d. 1749.
4 George Healey of Burringham, 1692-1772.
5 An Anthony Dempster of Brigg, possibly a solicitor, occurs in title deeds of the 1730's and 1740's.
6 Sir Nevil Hickman (1701-32), 4th Bart. of Gainsborough.
7 Joseph Hoole, Vicar of Haxey, 1712-36; rector of St. Ann's, Manchester, 1736-45.
8 The text appears to be "Presi" followed by a superior 'l'. 'Presidential' would fit. The *New English Dictionary* cites a seventeenth century use of the term "presidential episcopacy", so possibly 'presidential' could be applied to a high church supporter of episcopal supremacy. (Sir Francis Hill in *Georgian Lincoln*, p. 25, transcribes the word as "Presbyterian").
9 Albermarle Bertie (d. 1742), a brother of the 1st Duke of Ancaster, had been soundly defeated by Sir William Massingberd in the last contested election for the county, following the death of Sir Willoughby Hickman in 1720.

Sleeford, Feb. 4th 1723/4

13.

If you please to send Ned to Mr. Barnes's, Book-keeper at the Red Lyon in Aldersgate Street he will Pay you twenty pounds. I shall receive twenty-five pounds of George Dickinson in a Week's time; then I shall have an opportunity of sending you some more money.

My Master's Interest and Creditt engages me to go about this County to serve Mr. Viner, and now I am going to Spalding and Boston and amongst Sir John Meres's tenants at Kirton,[1] and Alderkirk[2] in Holland, to make all the Interest I can for him. I shall be at Harpswell Next Thursday and then expect to meet with a letter from you, for I have not received one these three weeks.

[P.S.] The Election will be the 12th Instant and I believe Sir Nevil will loose it. Pray look in the Advertisements in the Prints of Thursday and Saturday next.

[Asw. 10/27/12]

1 Kirton in Holland.
2 Algarkirk.

14.
Harpswell, Feb. 15th 1723/4

I am very glad that you received the twenty pounds, which my last letter advised you of, and as soon as I can, I'll send you more. My Master is gone this day to dine at Scawby[1] with Mr. Maddison and his Lady, and to Morrow He leaves Harpswell in order to go with Colonel Saunderson for London, where you'll see him in a few days, and then He will give you a Particular Account of the Election. I hope you received that line I sent you by Colonel Saunderson's Servant who set out of Lincoln Post Immediately after Mr. Viner was Chaired. Wee all Rejoyce very much for our Success and believe now it is not in the Power of the Torys ever to Chuse another Member for our County.[2]

As soon as the weather is a little Temperate I hope you'll come home, for here you'll find more advantage from the Air in one day than in a Month where you are. Your best way of coming down will be (I think) to hire a Coach to Stamford and travel as far every day as may be performed with Ease and Pleasure to you, and, when you have Rested yourself three or four days or a week at Mr. Maddison's, you may then borrow his Coach to Harpswell.

My Master has run no Hazard in Soliciting Sir John Meres's Tenants, for Sir John gave him an Express order so to do before I went into the Fen, which order I took with me to Confirm what I requested of them. I hope every thing that is Acted will be as Satisfactory to Sir John as to the Rest of the Gentlemen who has an interest in this Country and Employed it for the Service of Mr. Viner.

I'll take all the care I can of Mr. Maddison and Mrs. Maddison if they please to call at Harpswell in their way home, the best Bed being set up for their Reception; which is all at Present.

[P.S.] I did not receive Mrs. Betty's Answer to my last, nor any letter either from yourselfe or Her since the Ninth of January last.

[Endorsed] Febr. 15th. Money £20

[Asw. 10/27/13]

¹ About 10 miles North of Harpswell, seat of the Nelthorpe family. Sir Henry Nelthorpe, 4th Bart., died, aged 11, in 1729, and was succeeded by his uncle, Sir Henry, 5th Bart., d. 1746.

² The result of the Lincolnshire election was Vyner, 2584 votes, Hickman 2406.

Harpswell Feb. 29th 1723/4

15. [*Possibly to Elizabeth Whichcot*]

I am very much Concerned Madam that my Mistress is attended with a Fever and Ague, which certainly now must be very Violent, coming after such a Severe illness, but I hope your next will give a Better Account of her Health.

I shall send as much Money as I can Possibly raise by the Lincoln Carrier next Munday Seven-Night, and will Continue to lett my Mistress have all the money that comes to my hands, as I receive it, till I hear of her coming down.

I have paid all my Mistress's bills that she left, except Mr. Coal's, Mr. Wooldry and John Harrison.¹ I left them till the last because they want money the least of any Tradesmen wee deal with. As to sending a Particular of my Accounts, they are too large for a Post letter, but upon the ballance there is Money due to me. I have received all her rents but John Codd, £5 10s., and Peter Grainger, £28. The first I shall receive in a day or two but the last sum I can't get till the Spring Marketts, that he sells some Sheep and Beasts to Pay with. There is no danger of looseing any money by Peter at Present, though it will be long before he can Pay. I expect that Mr. Maddison and his Lady will lye at Harpswell next Munday Night in their Way to Ketton and when I see Mrs. Maddison I'll deliver your Message. Since the Election Gainsborough People are very Silent but for their former Insolence they will have (I believe) some Soldiers Quartered amongst them.

Here is no News in this Neighbourhood worth the Notice, otherwise you should have had a Particular Relation of it.

[P.S.] I have got the best Bed up for Mr. Maddison and his Lady and have Borrowed a Fire-Grate and will Entertain them as well as I can till they leave Harpswell, and the Post after, I'll give you a Particular Account who came to see them and how everything was managed.

[Asw. 10/27/14]

¹ There is a receipt in 1724 for payment for groceries supplied by Richard Wooldray (Asw. 2/102/15).

16.

Mr. Maddison and his Lady was at Harpswell Munday Night, Tuesday and Tuesday Night, and went away Wednesday after Breakfast. They seemed pleased with the Entertainment they met with, and I don't doubt but they will give you some Account of it and return you their thanks. They had Partridges of Ranger's geting at Harpswell, and I gave them a Dick [*sic* for duck] home with them.

Mr. Nelthorpe[1] and his two Sons was here with them whilst they stayed. William Dickinson and his Wife Supped with them of Munday Night. The Two Mr. Bassetts[2] and Mr. Athorpe[3] dined with them of Tuesday, and Joseph Dickinson and his Wife Supped with them of Tuesday Night. Most of the Neighbours came to see them and drank Tee, which Mrs. Maddison brought along with her.
[? Incomplete]
[Endorsed] March, Money £30. I think 1723
[Asw. 10/27/16]

[1] Probably the Henry Nelthorpe who succeeded to the baronetcy in 1729. Cf. no. 14 n. 1.
[2] The Bassetts were a great clerical family in the area in the eighteenth and nineteenth centuries. William (c. 1663-1729) was at this time vicar of Glentworth and curate of Harpswell. His son Ralph (1700-40) was vicar of Corringham, about four miles West of Harpswell from 1724 to his death. A younger son William (1703-65), vicar of Glentworth and Archdeacon of Stow, married Elizabeth Whichcot in 1730.
[3] Robert Athorp (d. ? 1744), rector of Springthorpe, about 4 miles West of Harpswell.

Harpswell, March 21st 1723/4
17.

I am glad you received the £30 according to the Notice I gave you of it, and the Carriage is always a Shilling for every ten pounds. As to forty pounds which you desire more, I will take care to send it as soon as any Money comes into my hands that will answer the Sum. Your designe of taking a whole Coach is much the Best and Easiest way for you to get Home and, if you don't call at Ketton, the Charge of coming to Harpswell in the same Coach will not be a great deal more than to Lincoln. By the latter end of April you may venture to travel without any Danger of Cold if the Weather be any thing tolerable. I will take care to get your Bed Curtains doubled and observe directions as to the Length, and also about the Chamber door to keep out cold. I will be sure to get Wine and Sack and Ale for you against you come to Harpswell and some Oyl at the Mart. If you would have any Anchoveys, Capers or Blues, be pleased to give me your orders, and I will buy them at the Mart.
I hope Madam by this time you have so far Resolved of a Journey to Harpswell that you have agreed with Mr. Blackburn for a Coach and fixed the time of Coming out of Town, which I shall be very glad to hear and will keep it very private. Your ewes are now about lambing and some of the lambs will be fit to Kill against your Coming down. Richard and John Harvey are very busie Gardening, and wee shall have them in good order now in a little time. Wee have had very great Rains lately but the Weather begins now to Clear up. A Month of fine weather will make the Roads very good and it will be very pleasant travelling, which is all at Present.
[Endorsed] March 21st. About £30.
[Asw. 10/27/15]

Lincoln, Apr. 6th 1724

18.

I have Paid to Mr. Barnes for you the Forty Pounds which you may have the Night you Receive this or the next Morning, as you Please to send, Mr. Barnes having given his Book-keeper an order by this Post to Pay the Money as soon as you send for it. I hope Madam you hold your Resolution of leaving London the 13th of this Instant, as (I Presume) you have agreed with Mr. Blackburn.[1] I'll take care to have every thing that's Necessary for your Reception and heartily wish you a Plesant Journey.

[Asw. 10/27/17]

[1] Among the vouchers for 1724 is one for the payment on Apr. 18th of £13 10s. to John Blackburn for the hire of himself and his coach; five days from London to Harpswell and four days returning. (Asw. 2/102/10).

Ketton, June 14th 1724

19. *To Madam Whichcot at Harpswell*

I got to Ketton of Fryday Night where I found Mr. Maddison and his Lady and Miss in Perfect Health. The family had been in the Greatest Concern for fear he should have had the Small Pox but was soon Happily convinced that his Disorder was only the Measles which he was very full of. In the Height of the Distemper, when even the Doctor assured him it was the Small Pox, he was not the least affrighted or fearfull of himselfe, but was Extreamly troubled that the Distemper would Reach his Lady and Little one, and the fatal Consequence that might attend it; but thank God, Happy are they that it is otherwise and that they may be ever so is the Sincere wish

of

Your Most Faithfull and

Obedient Servant.

[P.S.] Of Tuesday Night I hope to be at Harpswell. Miss is a very fine Child and Joyns with her Pappa and Mamma in Duty to you and love and Service to Mrs. Bett.

Mr. John Whichcot is now here and sends his Duty also. He complains (as all the World else does) very much of Poverty and, without any Preface to his demands, says I must leave him a Guinea, which I durst not but submitt to, Concidering the Horse-course and the Assemblys at Stamford, and we both hope Madam you won't be Angry at it.

[Endorsed] June 24th 1724

[Asw. 10/27/18]

Harpswell, Nov. 20th 1725

20.

I had sooner wrote to [have] Acquainted you with my Master's Return to Harpswell and the good Encouragement he met with from

Sir John[1], but he told me he had done it before. Therefore I deferred writing till this Post, in hopes to have given you as Good an Account of his last Journey, but can't do it. The Mother is now Extreamly against it, and the Young One Appears very shy[2]: my Master bears all this with a great deal of Spiritt, and is resolved to be at Louth Assembly on Munday Seven-night again. There is some talk as though the Estate can't be sold till the Young Lady comes to age, which my Master will Endeavour to be well satisfied of and, if true, the affair will be soon Concluded, for I find Love's greatest efforts can't the least taint his Reason or make him Guilty of an Indiscreet Act. Yesterday my Master and Mr. Scrope dined at Harpswell and went after dinner into the Isle, and designes to dine of Sunday with Sir Thomas Saunderson,[3] who came to Glentworth with his Lady[4] last Night, with an Intent (as I hear) to stay there till Candlemas. Mrs. Tancred and her Two Nieces comes to Glentworth, along with Miss Saunderson, next week. If, Madam, you do not like the Malt drink where you are, be pleased to give me an order and I will send you a Hogshead of the Best Ale I can get in Lincoln, and send it Immediately by way of Linn. I have Received no bills from Cambridge, but will write to Mr. John Whichcot to send them, and I'll take care to discharge them.

[P.S.] My Mother Presents Her Humble service to your selfe and Miss Betty, which concludes this.

[Asw. 10/24/9]

[1] Presumably Thomas Whichcot had been sounding Sir John Meres' attitude to his proposed marriage.
[2] The name of the object of his courtship is never given. Cf. no. 22 n. 5.
[3] Colonel Saunderson was created a K.B. on 27th May 1725.
[4] He married Frances, daughter of George, 1st Earl of Orkney.

Harpswell, Dec. 4th 1725

21.

I am glad you have Received Ten Pounds from Knot, which I paid yesterday to Alderman Brown[1]: it will serve you some time for Tea and Wine. I would not have you, Madam, be at the Trouble of sending to such trifling Fellows for Money, but, if Sir Horrace[2] would please to Enquire at Norwich, who would take Twenty or Thirty Pounds at London and send me an Order to whom I shall Pay it, I can get William Dickinson to pay it in a Fortnight or three Weeks time, and you might take it at Norwich. This, I believe, will be the Easiest and the best way of serving you. I have ordered two halfe Hogsheads of Ale, directed for Sir Horrace, to be left with Mr. Taylor, Wine Merchant, in Linn and will write Mr. Taylor a line to take care of them and send them forward, but when they will be at Norwich, Mr. Taylor must let Sir Horrace know that by a letter. I hope they will come safe to you before Christmas and prove very good, but, in the mean time, you should Drink Wine at your Meal if you dislike the Malt Liquer. Last Munday my Master went to Louth Assembly and I have neither Seen nor heard from him since, and this is Saturday Noon, so that I can't say one word of that Affair. I have not heard as yet from Mr. John Whichcot; I suppose they stay to put in the Christmas Quarter, before they'll send his bills, which I will take care to Pay very soon after I receive them. Mr. John has been so little in College this six or seven months last past, that, I begg leave to say, I hope his stay at Rackheath won't Exceed the Holy-days. Last Thursday George Dickinson paid me Twenty five Pounds on Mr. John's Account. He had just been Collecting Rents at Scotton[3] and all the Tenants told him they heard Sir John had given that Estate to Mr. Whichcot, and that Mr. Whichcot (their new Landlord, as they call'd him) was going to be Married; I heartily wish it was true. I'm glad Miss Betty is so happy in such Fine Cousins: She is Capable of Following every good Example, and I don't doubt but now she will. I'm mightily pleased your Company has made Lady Pettus look better: I hope hers has not made you look worse. Our great Neighbours have not had many visitors; most of their Company as yet have been Stewards. Lady Frances has no Companion with her; she spends her time pritty much with Miss. Her Ladyship and Sir Thomas goes next Tuesday to Lincoln Assembly, and my Master with them, which Concludes all the News that has Comed to the Knowledge of your most Obedient and most Humble Servant.

[P.S.] My Master Received your letter which he gave me to Read and was mightily pleased with your kind Expressions and that Maternal Affection which attended every line. At his Return he will Answer it. I'm sorry, Madam, that my letters are so short; it is not Idleness, but the want of knowing more, that Occasions it. Peter, who joyns with me in Duty to you, is a brave Boy. I think, Madam, he now does, and I hope he will always, merit your Ladyship's Favour and Friendship. He never Challenges home but of Saturday Nights, and that upon force for a Clean shirt.[4]
My Mother Beggs your Acceptance of her Most Humble Service.
[Asw. 10/24/12]

---

[1] Hezekiah Browne (d. 1739), a mercer, mayor of Lincoln 1712, 1726. He was a younger son of a family who owned the manor of Yawthorpe in Corringham.
[2] Sir Horatio Pettus (cf. no. 8 n. 1).
[3] Meres owned the manor of Scotton about 12 miles N.W. of Harpswell.
[4] i.e., he never goes home, except on Saturday nights, to get a clean shirt. Who Peter was, I do not know.

Harpswell, Dec. 15th 1725

22. *Madam Whichcot at the Honoured Sir Horatio Pettus's Bart. at Rackheath, to be left at the Post-house in Norwich, Norfolk. By Caxton Bagg.*
I Promised in my last to give you an Account in this letter how

my Master's affairs stand with Relation to Miss —, but I dare not stay till an Opportunity offered, least you should think me Remiss in my Duty. The Night I wrote last to you he came home without knowing any thing Particular and is this day gone again to Louth Assembly, with a Resolution now to be satisfied whether the Young Lady and her Mother will accept of him or not. He will stay amongst them till Saturday or Sunday next and, at His Return home, will write to you himselfe. Notwithstanding that, I won't omitt any opportunity of Writing that will give you Satisfaction. I have given Mr. John Whichcot the trouble of a letter to wish him a good Journey to Rackey, and desired all his bills, that I may pay what's due to the College on his Account, and set him Clear in the World against his Return to Cambridge. My Master was at Home all the last Week, and had with him Mr. George Hennage,[1] Mr. Vincent Grantham[2] and two other Young Gentlemen near Lowth called Mr. Newtons.[3] Mr. Hennage had his Fox-Hounds, his Hunters, and his Servants at Spittle[4] and the Gentlemen lay at Harpswell. Mr. Hennage and one of the Newtons lay in the Second best Chamber which I made ready on Purpose, Mr. Grantham lay in the Bed in the Nursery, and the other Mr. Newton lay in the other Bed in the same Room. They was Extreemly well pleased both with their Diet and Lodging, all which we managed without borrowing. We had Entertained them Nicely, had Betty been here, for you can't but think we wanted a Cook. As to our Meat we had Beefe, Mutton, Rabbitts, Chickhans, Ducks, Gray Plover, Fieldfares, Larks, Codd, Cockles, Oysters, Pike, Eles, Lobster, Rice-milk and Puddings. Now Madam tho' here appears to be a great deal of Provision, yet when I tell you the Gentlemen had three hot meals every day for seven days and their Breakfasts (which was a Meal they mostly valued) always by Candlelight in a Morning, you can't think us Extravigant. Their Drink was mostly Ale, for all the time they was here they drank but four Bottles of Clarett. Wee are now as busie in washing the Linnen and Cleaning the Rooms, as wee was in taking care of the Gentlemen when they was here. I got Parry to be Chamber-maid, who Performed very carefully and well, and not the least damage happened to any Part of the Furniture. This Entertainment of my Master's was not Madam out of any Pure Affection he bears to those Gentlemen's Principles, but as they are Favoretts in the T — w — ll[5] Family; and, when his business is over there, his Inti[? macy wit]h those Friends of his will Terminate. Wee have lately Planted five and twenty Hundred of Ashes which my Master will have taken Care on at his Charge. There is a Sparrowgrass[6] Bed to be made in the Kitchen Garden; if you'll be at the Charge of it, you must let me know. It will Cost about twenty shillings or perhaps some little matter more. I have paid most of the Bills, and shall discharge all very soon. I can say nothing to you about Money till I have your Answer to my last letter. My

Mother Presents her Humble Service to you and Miss Betty, which is
all at Present.
[P.S.] My Master made your Complements to Sir Thomas Saunderson and Lady Frances, who took it very kindly.
[Asw. 10/24/2]

¹ George Heneage (1698-1745), of Hainton, 10 miles W. of Louth.
² Vincent Grantham (1693-1758), of Goltho, 10 miles N.E. of Lincoln.
³ A William Newton of Cockerington, near Louth, appears, together with the
Heneages, in the Lindsey register of papist's estates, 1719.
⁴ Spital in the Street, 2 miles E. of Harpswell, at the crossing of Ermine Street and
the Gainsborough—Louth road. Here was an almshouse; the court house of the vast
manor of Kirton in Lindsey, which was also used for Quarter Sessions; and an inn.
⁵ Tathwell, 3 miles S. of Louth, is the only Lincolnshire place name which fits.
It was the seat of the Chaplin family. According to Maddison's pedigrees (which may
be incomplete), the only available female member of this family was Frances, daughter of Porter Chaplin (d. 1719), and sister of Sir John Chaplin, 2nd Bart., who died
in 1730, aged 19. She was born in 1712, and, at 13, would have been a little young for
marriage in 1725.
⁶ Asparagus.

Harpswell, Dec. 22nd 1725

23.
    Your Letter came to me two or three days too late to pay you any
money by William Dickinson this Journey, but about four or five
Days after Christmas I shall Certainly pay you Twenty or Thirty
Pounds, but I can't be exact in the sum till I see Mr. John Whichcot's bills. My Master went yesterday to Lincoln Assembly with
Sir Thomas Saunderson and Lady Francis and told me he would
write to you by this Post, so you will be satisfied of his affairs, and
I begg leave to wish you a good Journey to Harpswell in the Spring.
I shall to morrow dispose of your kind Charity of Beafe to the Poor
of this place as usual, and I could wish that every body, According
to their Circumstances, would be as kind to the Needy; but the Rich-
est are the greatest Straingers to such a disposition. I let my Master
see your letter and he has promised to dine at home on New-year's
day, and wee shall (enabled by your kindness) Entertain him (I
hope) very well, which I'll give you an Account of, as soon as that
day is over. I heartily wish you a Merry Christmas and many of them.
[P.S.] My Mother presents her Humble service to your Ladyship and
Miss Betty and wishes you, and all the good Family, a Merry Christmas.
    I should have been more particular but I leave all news to my
Master.
    Wee are not doing anything in the Garden, but planting of Trees;
about the latter end of January wee shall nail the Trees, and so go
on doing what's Necessary. If Sir Horrace please to send his Method
of Managing his Grass and Gravel, wee will observe it as well as wee
can.
[Asw. 10/24/12]

c

Harpswell, Dec. 29th 1725

24.

I Received Mr. John Whichcot's Letter and his Bills last Sunday Night, though they were dated the fifteenth, but where they have loitered I can't tell. The Sum is £49 19s. 4¼d., which I have desired of Mr. Nichols to know where I shall Pay it at London. Here is none of Lady-day bills, which I desire Mr. John would send me down, that they may be regularly placed, and that I may know to what time he is Cleared. If the Money mentioned in my Master's letter be not paid to Mr. Hotchkish, I shall be very sorry and begg you'll not think the time long, nor me Neglegent, for, as soon as William Dickinson's Beasts goes, you shall have money, I having the sum by me Ready to repay him again. Christmas is very Dull at Harpswell and not yet begun at Glentworth, though their Common way of living is in great Plenty: Seventy stone of Beefe and about Two Quarters of Wheat is their Weekly stint for those two Articles of House keeping, by which you may guess at a Proportionable Quantity of other Provisions that they use. Their Tenants (I hear) are to be Entertain'd this Christmas to the Number of 300. This great living makes all sorts of Provision dearer than usual; last Munday Sil.[1] bought most of the Butter in this Neighbourhood at 6d a Pound, which made such Scarcity in Gainsborough Markett that butter Sold Readily at Seven pence a Pound. I'm glad wee have no Occation for any great Entertainments this Christmas.
[Rest torn off on other half of sheet.]
[Asw. 10/24/8]

---

[1] Presumably steward of the Saunderson household. The Whichcots bought their butter and cheese from William Dickinson (Asw. 2/102/13; 30).

Harpswell, Jan. 12th 1725/6

25.

The Favour of Miss Betty Whichcot's Letter by your order, that I Received about a Fortnight ago, should have been Answered long before this, had not the Post been stopped by the violence of the Frost and snow and the badness of the Roads, which (I don't doubt) you are in some measure sensible of. Here has not been a Post Boy since New Year's day, so that I could not tell you till now that my Master dined at Home and had William Dickinson, Henry Gildon, Thomas Lobley, Richard Stones,[1] and their wifes; they was very Merry, and drank Mr. John Whichcot's Health, and all at Rackey. The Day after, Sir Thomas Saunderson, Capt. Lumley, Mr. Bradshaw, Capt. Carey and Mr. Revell, one of Sir Thomas's Esquires, dined with my Master, and stayed till Eight at Night. They came out of Curiosity to see how my Master lived, and to Laugh at his Housekeeping. He gave them a Plum-Pudding, a Boyled Legg of Mutton, a Turkey, Minced Pyes and Tarts, which they seemed to like, by Eating heartily and being very Merry and Pleasant. Had it not been for the first and second Day of the New Year, wee had not known any thing of Christmas at Harpswell, but Glentworth is all Christmas. Sir Thomas has Entertained the Body of the Citty of Lincoln and Promissed to give them a Pair of Iron Gates and Pillars of Roach Abbie stone for their New Church in Lincoln,[2] which makes the Freemen Cry, "A Saunderson, a Saunderson". Of Saturday last, he had all his Tenants in this Neighbourhood and their Wifes, with whom Lady Frances was Extreamly diverted. Her Ladyship was last Munday Godmother to a child of Capt. Pownall's.[3] Now Madam I shall begg leave to tell you that Mr. Hudson Paid Twenty Pounds to Mr. Hotchkis for you, the 31st of December last, which I hope you have Received some time ago. I shall also Pay next Munday thirty Pounds to Mr. Nicol's order at London, and the Rest I will Return to him by Mr. Barnes. I will take all the Care I can, Madam, to make every Necessary Expence here as easie as Possible I can to you and will Return as much Money to you as you'd want (I hope) where you are. The Trees shall be Cut and Naled and the Sparrowgrass Bed made as soon as the Storm breaks. But sad is the Story I must tell you: our Great Assistant John Harvey is Dead; he fell sick upon the 4th of this month and dyed the 5th. I sent for his mother to come and bury him, but she was not able to endure the Journey, so she desired I would see him Decently Buryed, which accordingly I did, I'm sure Madam you are very Sorry, and so is my Master and every Body, for the loss of him and also for the suddenness of it. Wee have now no Body to doe any thing and as the Spring approaches wee shall want him more and more. Though, Madam, you can never expect to get his Fellow, you must have some Person in his place, but I shall not Enquire for one till I Receive your Orders. He dyed worth about thirty pounds which will be a great support to his Mother in her old Age. He was taken with an Aguish Fit and vomiting, which we thought was only the effect of Cold, that he was very subject to, but it ended fatally.

I'm sorry you had not Received the Ale. I heard long ago it was at Linn and I hope before this it is safe at Rackey, and proves good. Betty Stones was brought to bed the 3rd of this Instant of a Son and likely to do very well. My Master is very well and Presents his Duty, love and service where due, which, with my Mother's Humble service to your selfe and Miss Betty Whichcot, is all at Present. [Asw. 10/24/16]

[1] Presumably all Whichcot tenants.

[2] St. Peter at Arches. For his generosity Sir Thomas Saunderson received the freedom of the city (cf. Hill, *op. cit.*, 63-4).

[3] William Pownall (d. 1736) of Lincoln. Father of Thomas Pownall, Governor of Massachusetts.

Harpswell, Jan. 19th 1725/6

26.

The Honour of your last to me dated Jan. the 8th came not to Harpswell till the 18th, it being stopped I dare say by the badness of the Roads and Weather. I am glad your Ale is got safe to Rackey, but am surprised the Carriage from Linn to Norwich should be so Chargeable; it is a great deal more than from Lincoln to London. I desire Madam you would Pay board half yearly; it will be due about the 7th or 8th of May, at which time I shall have Money Ready to do it, but at Present I have paid so much Money, and have yet more to pay, that, Without Paying your Quarter's board, I shall be very much straightened, so desire it may be a halfyearly Payment. My Master thinks £100 is a Generous allowance for Mr. John Whichcot for all Charges whatever, and indeed Madam I think you had better do so than pay more, which hitherto you have done. My humble service attends Mr. John Whichcot and I wish him a good Journey to Cambridge. If you have Received £20 that I ordered for you by Mr. Hotchkish, and Mr. Dix's £10, you'll not want Pockett Money a long time. I'll pay Alderman Brown his £10 when I go next to Lincoln. Sir Thomas Saunderson, Lady Frances, etc., leaves Glentworth this Day. My Master will see them as far as Lincoln and will then Return home. He won't go to London, at the soonest, till towards Summer, and then will Call (I believe) at Rackey. You must now Madam stay from home (if your Health will give You leave) till you be the Right side your Debts, which, to the utmost of my Power and Care, shall be performed as soon as Possible. My Master sends his Duty, Love and Service, which, with My Mother's Humble service, Concludes this.
[Asw. 10/24/7]

Harpswell, Feb. 16th 1725/6

27.

I am Endeavouring to get a Young Country Fellow, that has been brought up to work and will be Ready and Willing to do what he is ordered, without finding fault and saying "this is not my Business". If I can get such a one, I hope it will be pleasing to you and my Master, whose advise and opinion I shall be sure to take. John Harvey's Livery I save for his Successor, and the Wages that was due to him, I have sent to his Mother; it was only for four Months. Richard has cut the Vines long since and is now busie in Cuting the Wall trees. The Grass, the Greens, and the Edgings must be taken care on, which shall be done at as little Expence as can be, but, as to the Gravel, it shall lye all Summer in Ridges as it now does. The House is very dry, and every fine morning wee let in the Sunshine to air the Rooms and the Furniture. Your Muff and Tuppitt has been often aired by the fire and are (I believe) as they should be. The

Chariott and Harness I get brushed over now and then, to prevent the Mould from doing any Prejudice to the Leather; the seats have been always within doors, and kept very Clean and dry. Mr. John Whichcot's Saddle and Bridle have been in your dressing Room ever since you left Harpswell, and not once used in all that time. As to the Agreement you Desire to put into an Article betwixt your selfe and Mr. John Whichcot, I have sent you a Copy of [it], which, if you like, it may be Executed; but my Master thinks there need no Article to oblige him to live within the Compass of such a Generous Allowance. I hope, Madam, Sir Horace will like to be paid halfe Yearly, because it shall be only for this one time; afterwards I will take Care to pay it Quarterly. The Tenants that are now in Arrears, being Kirk, Peter and some others, can't possibly pay till they sell what sheep this great Rot leaves them to go to April Fare with. Then I hope to have Money to serve both you and my Master, who lives very Reservedley at Home and, I believe, with much more satisfaction than the great ones about St. James's. He eats a Piece of Mutton or Beefe very heartily at Noon, and, after dinner, drinks the King's health and all his Friends at Rackey, in a Tankard and Toast. Thus Madam my Master lives, and is in such a thriving Condition that James Abraham has been here last Week to let out his Clothes. He presents his Duty, Love and Service where due, which concludes this.

[P.S.] I have paid Alderman Brown £10.

My Mother Presents her Humble Service to yourselfe and Miss Betty Whichcot.

Robert Codd's Child is to be Christened this day by the Name of Robert.

Memorandum   March 25th 1726
[Agreement that Mrs. Whichcot shall pay her son John Whichcot a yearly allowance of £100 for his expenses at Magdalene College, Cambridge, and shall herself receive the sum of £25 p.a. each, which he is being given by Sir John Meres and his brother Thomas Which-cot.]
[Asw. 10/24/10]

                                          Harpswell, Feb. 23rd 1725/6
28.

According to your Observation, letters are always five Days going or coming but never more, Unless the Post be stopped, which happened in the late Storm. However, so long as they don't miscarry, 'tis not much Matter. My last desired that your board might be paid half-yearly, for some very just Reasons which I gave, but, since you have paid the Quarter's, I will Endeavour to assist you with Money. This last ten Pounds which you have taken of Mr. Dix, I will discharge the next time I go to Lincoln, and whatever money you want more pray take it of the same Person and I'll take care to discharge it. Though Money is scarse with me at Present, a little time will make it more Plentiful. You seem to mention your Return with so much Resolution, that I am apt to think the end of this second Quarter is the time you have fixed in your own thoughts for your Return to Harpswell. It is at a time of the Year when the Days are long and the Roads generally good, therefore much Cheaper Traveling; but, as to your being better in your Circumstances for only halfe a Year's absence, can't possibly be Expected. Your expences at Harpswell have been so small this winter that they make a very little figure in the account, but your Charges Traveling two long Journeys in one halfe year is very Considerable. But I find Mrs. B[etty] is the Instrument of hastening you home; I'm affraid she will not in any place give you the Satisfaction by her behaviour that she ought as a Daughter, but I believe you may be the Easiest and most Secure with her at Harpswell. Her behaviour has given my Master such an ill opinion of her that I much question whether he will write to her or not, but yet I hope he will. As to my having the Parks or not, shall be as it Consists with your Conveniency; if you keep only a Pair of Mares and a Cow, whatever Stock I put in more I will Pay you for; as to sheep they are so very Rotten everywhere that whoever buys any this Spring must Run great Hazards. Mr. Bassetts[1] of Glentworth have been well all this winter, except William who has been ill of the Piles ever since you went. His disorder turned to be an Ulser, but will be cured without Cuting. Mr. Ralph and Miss Lidia[1] lives together at Corringham, and I believe he has almost rubbed off all Reflections that used to be whispered against him. The Old Madam Pelham[2] Dyed last Munday and Mr. Pelham (who is at London) is sent for to the Funeral. Mr. Draper of Brigg Embalmed her, that Mr. Pelham might have time to come down. I have got a young Man who was never in Service but Bred up Honestly and seems very willing to do every thing that he is ordered. I hired him of his Father, one John Fisher of Aisby;[3] his business is Jack of all trades. Mr. Nelthorpe[4] and his two Sons came here last Munday and stays till to Morrow. Mr. Waterworth[5] was also here Munday and Tuesday Night; wee have had long sits at Cards. They all Present their Duty, Love and Service. You'll have a letter from him by the next Post. Sir Francis Whichcot has sent to Invite him to Aswarby, but when he will go I can't tell. This, Madam, with my Mother's humble service to your selfe and Miss Betty, is all at Present.

[P.S.] I'm glad to heare Mr. John Whichcot is got to Cambridge. [Asw. 10/24/14]

---

[1] For the Bassett family cf. 16 no. 2.

[2] Probably the widow of Charles Pelham (c. 1635-92) of Brocklesby, and mother of the present Charles Pelham (cf. no. 9 n. 1).

[3] A hamlet in the parish of Corringham.

[4] It seems unlikely that this was Henry Nelthorpe, later 5th Bart., as he had no sons at this time (cf. no. 14 n. 1).
[5] Headmaster of Brigg Grammar School from 1716 to 1757. (Cf. F. Henthorn, *History of Brigg Grammar School*, pp. 40-46).

Harpswell, March 26th 1726

29.

I am very Sorry to hear your Cold has been so violent as to Confine you to your Chamber a week, but I hope by this time it has so Entirely left you as not to Return any more. In these parts Colds have been so general that very few have Escaped them in some degree or other, tho' I thank God my Master has Enjoyed good Health and brisk Hunting all this Winter. I have paid Mr. Brown two ten pounds but have not had an Opportunity to pay him the third since I Received your order, but will do it at his Return from Norwhich. The thirty Pounds that you'll want in the beginning of May, I will Endeavour to Return to you by Mr. Hotchkish of London, or, if you can have it of Mr. Brown's Friend, I'll Pay Mr. Brown here upon the first notice that you have Received it. I shall also Clear every thing upon Mr. John Whichcot's Account the next month, and will then begin to Pay him according to your Agreement. I am Concerned to hear those Complaints of Mrs Betty, but sure Madam your Indulgence (or Nothing) will make her Dutyful. I still hope my Master will write a Letter of advise to her, and, if that has no effect upon her future behaviour and Conduct, it will then put him to a Stand to know what more to do. Glentworth Hall is now Inhabited as it used to be, by Mr. Bursey, one Maid, a Huntsman, and Boy; the Rest are either at London or Sandbeck.[1] The upper Park shall be Meadowed for you, and the Lower Park, my Master and my selfe will pay Rent for till your Return. I will enquire in Summer for a Mare to Match Harrison[2]; for Jenney Mare will never be fit for any thing now so well as Breeding, for which business my Master has partly bought her of me for Six Guineas if you be willing, the Price being six shillings more than you gave for her, above five years ago. I am very glad Madam you are Resolved to stay at Rackey till August; it will be much better for your affairs, and, if Mrs Betty does but perform her Promises to you, it will make you spend your time with Pleasure. I will take the Best season for laying in Coals and Lock them up till you come. Our Assizes ended yesterday at Lincoln, when the High Sherriffe, Mr. Stovin[3], and about Thirty of my Master's Friends along with him, dined at Harpswell in their Return home. The High Sheriffe appeared very Hansomly and had his liveries which was Blue neatly trimmed with Silver lace upon their Wastcoats. My Master is also writing to you, so that the Rest of the News I shall leave for him to entertain you with.

[P.S.] According to your order I will waite of Mrs Anderson: Miss Anderson has been in London with Mrs Pelham about three weeks.

My Mother Presents her Humble Service to your selfe and Miss Betty Whichcot.
[Asw. 10/24/4]

1 The Yorkshire seat of the Earls of Scarbrough.
2 Harrison was the name of the horse. There is a bill of John Dewick for black-smith's work, including shoeing "Harrison mare", "Jenny mare" and "Betty mare" in 1724. (Asw. 2/102/28).
3 James Stovin (? 1678-1739) of Crowle in the Isle of Axholme.

Harpswell, April 9th 1726
30.   [*Thomas Whichcot to his mother*]
I'm very sorry my Letter, which I wrote a Post or two before Sir Francis, has miscarried. I wish this may have better luck, and to that end I have made Wallace direct it and seal it with his Seal, least my Hand and Seal should be the Reason of its not arriving safe. I am mighty glad to find you approve of the Company I have invited to your House; in my last I asked pardon for the Liberty I had taken. When I wrote before, it was just after the Assizes and I told you some news from thence which now is old, and therefore won't trouble you with it. However I must lett you know the Honour the High-Sheriff did me in his return home from Lincoln to the Isle, that he and about 30 more of that Island dined with me and were very merry great part of the Afternoon. I went last Monday to Sir John Tyrwhit's and returned yesterday. He was very merry and cheerful as ever I've known him, but has turned away almost all his servants, and is in such a bad name for a pationate Master that he can't gett any more hereabouts. He'll be oblig'd to you if you'll transport him some over the Wash. I hear my Brother Maddison has burid his Mother: I write this Post, to condole with him. I have had a letter from my Uncle to invite me to London: I thank him heartily but I don't intend to stir this year so far from Home, unless it be for a Week or 10 days to wait on you at Rackheath. I don't know how long Sir Francis will stay here. I believe (however I thank you) we shall want nothing out of your Store Room. I begg you'll distribute my Duty, Love and Service where due, and believe me to be, Madam,

Your most dutyfull son
and Obedient Humble Servant,
T. Whichcot

[P.S.] I shall be glad to hear from you that my Sister behaves herselfe well and discreetly, for I want very much to be reconciled to her but, without her entire alteration in her Conduct and behaviour, I'm affraid I never shall; and therefore, if you can send me that good News, do. Sir Francis and his Lady send their Service to you and thanks for your Letter.
[Asw. 10/24/11]

Harpswell, May 7th 1726

31.

I understand by a line I had the other day from Alderman Brown, that Mr. Dix has paid you Thirty Pounds, which I will Pay next Week to the Alderman, though by that time I may have your orders for it. I have also Paid Twenty five Pounds to Mr. John Whichcot by Mr. Barnes, but have not as yet been told by him that he has Received it. Every Payment and Demand on your Account I shall always very Strictly observe, but Rents as yet comes in very Easily.

Sir Francis Whichcot and his Lady left Harpswell last Sunday and are at Mr. Banks's[1] house in Lincoln, where they intend to stay till next Wednesday and then set forward for London. Her Ladyship said when she left us that she was much better for coming to Harpswell, and went away very well pleased. She will (I suppose) Travel so slowly, that when she comes to Stamford she'll Stay there three or four days and then proceed till she is tired again. She is so weakly that it will be very Extraordinary if ever she lives to see Aswarby, but if she recovers she will come to Harpswell to Return you thanks for all your Favours and Invite you to her House at Aswarby. I have taken down, and brushed and foulded up the Bed Curtains and Window Curtains in the best Room and put every thing as it was before, and hope I shall have no more Occation to meddle with them till your Return.

I hope Mrs. Betty has Received my letter that gave her an Account that I had sent her Blue and White Gown and the top of the Pettycoat to Mrs. Nobbes,[2] which will be at London this day. I only told her she was to Clean it, the other orders was to come from Mrs. Betty. I should oftner trouble you with letters, but there is no news offers here worth sending so far; the best I have (which is very good) is that my Master Enjoys a Perfect state of Health and stays much at home, unless when Publick business calls him away. He has been four or five times upon the Commission of Sewers, and is to meet the Commissioners again next Wednesday. He takes a deal of Pains to Understand the method of Proceeding, and will (I dare say) soon be a master of it. He Presents his Duty, Love and service which concludes this.

[P.S.] I am very sorry Madam to tell you your Jenney Mare foaled a Dead Foal; the Mare Recovers and I have got her Served again. Wee are here Madam so burnt up with a Scorching Sun, and [rest torn off]

[Asw. 10/24/3]

---

[1] Joseph Banks II (1695-1741) of Revesby, who was tenant of a Dean and Chapter house in the close of Lincoln. He was Sir Francis Whichcot's brother-in-law.

[2] There are a number of vouchers for haberdashery bought from Thomas Nobbs and his wife in London. (e.g., Asw. 10/32/2).

Harpswell, Oct 1st 1726

32.

Though I have not the Honour to Receive any Commands or Orders from you, you'll expect to be Informed how all does here, my Master and Mr. John Whichcot being now both at Harpswell and in very good Health. Indeed, I have said Amiss that my Master is now at Harpswell, for he went yesterday Morning to Doncaster Commission[1] and from thence designes to visit Sir Thomas Saunderson and (I believe) will Stay with him till he comes to Glentworth. Mr. John's not getting his Clothes in time prevented his going into Yorkshire. Mr. Banks was to be at the Commission and to go Post from thence into Buckinghamshire to attend that Mournful Solemnity of Lady Whichcot's Funeral, which is to be next Munday. Sir Francis has acquainted my Master with his great loss, and my Master is now in Mourning for her Ladyship. Mr. John Whichcot's Duty, Love, and Service, with my Mother's Humble Service Concludes this.

[P.S.] Your Return to Harpswell is Expected and hoped for every week.

[Asw. 10/24/15]

1 Commission of Sewers.

Harpswell, April 19th 1727

33. [Address torn off, but presumably same as 35]

I shall be very glad to hear that Mrs. Maddison is brought to Bed of a Boy and does well, and, by the time that Mr. Wallis and Mr. Newcomen[1] comes to Ketton, I shall have money to send. If I have it sooner, it shall sooner be with you. I'll take care that N. shall be discouraged at Harpswell and will Endeavour to prevent his coming to live in this Neighbourhood. I'm sorry there should still continue to be any reason for those Complaints you make of —; sure, good advise and time will discover to her selfe her own Great Indiscretion; till then, all the Reasoning in the World will (I'm affraid) prove Fruitless. I could fill all this paper with Answering yours but had Rather chuse to be silent till I have an opportunity of doing it more Securely. Mr. Anderson has been ill of an Ague and Fever but is upon the Recovery and Lady Mary Saunderson[2] leaves Buxton next Tuesday and Lady Margarett Monson[3] very soon, in order to Lye in at London; which is all the News at Present.

[P.S.] My Mother Presents her Humble Service to yourselfe, Mr. Maddison and his Lady, and Mrs Betty, and Heartily wishes and Prays for Mrs. Maddison having a good Time and a Boy.

[Asw. 10/24/5]

1 Possibly Theophilus Newcomen of Lincoln, d. 1741, but this was a family of vast ramifications in the county.

[2] Lady Mary Saunderson (d. 1737), eldest daughter of Lewis Watson, 1st Earl of Rockingham and widow of Wray Saunderson (c. 1680–c. 1707) grandson of George Saunderson, 5th Viscount Castleton.

[3] Lady Margaret Monson (1696-1752), wife of Sir John Monson (c. 1693-1748), 5th Bart., and 1st Baron Monson from 1728. She was the youngest daughter of the 1st Earl of Rockingham.

London, Apr. 20th 1727

34. *Thomas Whichcot to his mother*

I return you thanks for the Favour of your last and am mighty glad to find by it that you are in such good Health, which I wish may continue. I am concerned to hear that your Companion is not yett come to her senses. I'm affraid she never will and therefore how can I, with either Honour or Honesty, recommend her to a Man that I have any vallue for? As to the Business about your House, which you are so kind as to consult me in, I protest I can't tell how to decide. The Case stands thus with me: I am very sorry that you have a Mind to quit the House, and so I am to find it is such an Expence to you. I have no Mind to lett a Lease of it to any Stranger because, if I marry, I have no where then to bring a wife to, and yett I have no Mind to marry without a Probability of Maintaining a wife handsomely. So that you see upon casting up these Considerations it stands thus—I desire that you may enjoy what you have pleasantly, but yet I have no mind to lay my self under any great Inconveniency. I have an Inclination to marry but yett I'm affraid to running into Debt after it. This is my Case as it now stands, which I verily believe nothing but matrimony can cure, and I have very good Reason to think I can have the Remedy: a young Lady (whom you know very well and her whole Family) and will have 5000 Pounds paid down.[1] Now here is my case with a Lady and fortune which, if you'll please to state and make it appear in your next to me that you like it, and how I may live comfortably afterwards, I'll set about it immediately. Or if you have any other Method of Living to propose, I am ready to oblige you. I desire that this may be private between you and Sister Maddison, who I think will be a sincere and good Confidant and Counsellour in this Grand Affair of Life. I beg you'll present my Duty, Love and Service where due, and wish my Sister a happy Minute[2] and Recovery. I hope to have an Answer to this very shortly. I am in great Hast to conclude, or else I shall lose the Post, who am, Madam,

Your most Dutyful Son and Obedient Servant.

[Asw. 10/24/17]

[1] His first wife was Eliza Maria (1710-33), daughter of Francis Anderson of Manby, on 27th Nov. 1729.

[2] i.e., a safe delivery.

Harpswell, May 10th 1727
35. *To Madam Whichcot at John Maddison's Esq., at Ketton near Stamford*

Your two last letters came to my hands within a Day of each other, tho' there was ten Days' Difference in their dates. Where the first of them was stopt I can't tell, but however neither of them was broke open. I am very glad that Mrs. Maddison and the Child are both well. I heartily wish her a Perfect Recovery and a Boy next time. I went yesterday to Lincoln on Purpose to talk with Mr. Dixon[1] about his Coach coming for you the last Week of this Month; which he will very carefully do for three Pounds ten shillings. He is gone this Morning with Part of Sir John Monson's Family into the South and will be at home again next Wednesday; at which time I have promised to meet him at Lincoln to make a Punctual Bargain with him in Writing, if you give me an Answer to this Immediately (else I shall not get it in time) that you are Resolved to come home, and have fixed your day for the Coach to be at Ketton for you. I have Enquired very much about Lodgings, but can find none without some of those Inconveniencys you can't put up with. I have not yet done Enquiring, but shall give you a farther Account by the next Post. I am sure you'll want Money and therefore I must venture twenty Pounds again by the Newsman, and whatever more you'll want may come when you leave Ketton. As no place is more Pleasant, so none is of more advantage to your Health than Harpswell, and, so long as you Please to stay at it, I'll take all the Care in My Power to make every Expencive Article in House-Keeping as Moderate and easie as Possible to you and don't in the least doubt but My Master will be willing to pay for his own and his servants Board. My Mother's Humble Service Concludes.

[P.S.] Mr. Carter of Brigg and his Family are going to live upon his Estate at Redbourne,[2] and have fitted up a House for that Purpose, therefore 'tis Probable you might now Board with Mrs. Dempster. Sir John Monson, his Lady, etc., have left Burton this Morning.
[Asw. 10/24/6]

[1] An agreement by William Dixon to bring Mrs. Whichcot home from Ketton with a coach and four horses, for £3 10s. is among the vouchers (Asw. 2/103/7). This was considerably cheaper than the journey to Ketton in December 1726, performed by John Young of Stamford for £6 (Asw. 2/103/8).

[2] William Carter of Bathafern, Denbighshire, inherited the Redbourne estate, about 10 miles N.E. of Harpswell, at the beginning of the century. His son Robert assumed the additional surname of Thelwall, and the estate descended, through Robert's daughter, to the Dukes of Saint Albans.

SOME CORRESPONDENCE OF
JOHN FARDELL, DEPUTY REGISTRAR
1802-1805

EDITOR'S NOTES

The original grammar and spelling have been retained, though some abbreviations have been extended, many capitals have been lowered and punctuation has been inserted or varied. The 'Dear Sir' at the beginning and the subscription at the end have been omitted, as have the addresses on letters to Fardell, all of which are addressed to him at Lincoln. Some of the letters have been damaged by damp and are partly missing. Where the document is missing, the fact is indicated, e.g. [torn]. Where words are illegible, the mark ... is used. Words which have been supplied are in square brackets. The letters from John Fardell are all drafts and have a good many alterations and deletions, and the final version only has been given. The correspondence is clearly incomplete.

All manuscripts cited are in the custody of the Lincolnshire Archives Office unless otherwise stated. Wills cited as at Somerset House have since been transferred to the Public Record Office.

I wish to thank Miss Kathleen Major, the Society's Editor, for drawing my attention to these letters and their significance.

INTRODUCTION

Office-holding under the crown has been recognized as a subject significant not only for the study of English administrative history, but also for its wider bearing on the whole structure of politics and society. Less attention has been paid to the officials who served under the church, who discharged a multitude of functions which could be deputed by bishop, by archdeacon, or by dean and chapter or other peculiar jurisdiction. The small file of letters transcribed here, preserved among the registrars' correspondence in the Lincoln diocesan records and listed as Cor. R. 6, provides a glimpse of the actual functioning of one particular ecclesiastical office at the beginning of the nineteenth century and illustrates some long-established characteristics of office-holding in the church.[1]

The late fifteenth and early sixteenth centuries saw the development of new attitudes towards public office in both central government and church. Offices were regarded less as a form of service and obligation to a superior authority than as pieces of property which could be bought and sold, leased and mortgaged, or given as provision for children, and possession of which entitled the holder to the exploitation of their profits. The conception of an office as a freehold property which, it has been argued, derived originally from the ecclesiastical definition of a benefice, now came to be more nearly applied.[2] In the church this changed attitude is associated with the rise of a new class of professional ecclesiastical lawyers, many of whom were no longer ecclesiastics as in the middle ages, and whose remuneration could therefore no longer take the form of preferment to benefices. Instead the lay, married officials were given security of tenure by patents of appointment for life, or even achieved heredity by patents for more than one life, in appointments which had earlier been granted during pleasure or good behaviour.[3] In the diocese of Lincoln ecclesiastical officials held their offices for term of their life or for more than one life, almost without exception, by the second half of the sixteenth century. Patents of office granted by bishops and archdeacons were still being granted for these terms in

---

[1] Characteristics which survived into the early nineteenth century when the whole system was described on the eve of reform in *Returns of all Courts which exercise Ecclesiastical Jurisdiction and of all Courts which exercise Peculiar and Exempt Jurisdiction in England and Wales* (1828) and in *Reports of the Commissioners on the Practice and Jurisdiction of the Ecclesiastical Courts of England and Wales* (1832).

[2] Christopher Hill, *Economic Problems of the Church from Archbishop Whitgift to the Long Parliament* (1956), pp. 52-53; K. W. Swart, *Sale of Offices in the Seventeenth Century* (The Hague, 1949), pp. 83, 112, 113.

[3] On this change in some ecclesiastical offices, *see* K. Major, 'The Office of Chapter Clerk at Lincoln', *Medieval Studies presented to Rose Graham* (Oxford, 1950), pp. 163-88; Colin Morris, 'The Commissary of the Bishop in the Diocese of Lincoln', *Journal of Ecclesiastical History*, X (1959), 63; B. L. Woodcock, *Medieval Ecclesiastical Courts in the Diocese of Canterbury* (Oxford, 1952), pp. 39, 104.

the early nineteenth century, though among offices granted by the
Dean and Chapter of Lincoln a change back from life-tenure to tenure
during good pleasure had taken place in almost all offices.[1]

The patent offices which are the subject of these letters were those
of Registrars under the Bishop's Commissary in the Archdeaconries
of Lincoln and Stow. In the post-Reformation diocese of Lincoln,
before its reduction in the nineteenth century, there were thirteen
registrarships: the Principal Registrar of the diocese, and, in each of
the six archdeaconries, a registrar under the Bishop and his Commissary, and a registrar under the Archdeacon and his Official,
though in practice certain of these offices were often combined.
Whereas, according to canon 127, the judicial offices of Chancellor,
Commissary, and Official must be held by qualified lawyers of twenty-
six years or more, with at least the degree of M.A. or LL.B.,[2] there
was no rule requiring registrars or their deputies to have any particular education or to have reached a certain age. Consequently
bishops and archdeacons, anxious to provide for kinsmen and
friends who were without professional qualifications, found it convenient to bestow registrarships. Registrarships were also the offices
in which grants for a term longer than the life of the grantee were
most common. According to the canons of 1640, no patent should be
granted to Chancellor, Commissary, or Official for longer than the
life of the grantee, and no reward should be taken for any such
office.[3] From the late seventeenth century onwards in the diocese
of Lincoln, patents of these offices were made to one grantee only,
for term of his life. Registrarships, however, were granted for two or
three lives from the early seventeenth century. The most usual form
which had developed by the eighteenth century was to two or three
persons jointly for term of their lives and the life of the longest lived
of them. Patents in this form might be a method of granting a reversion to the second person rather than of sharing an office. In practice
the provision in most patents that the office might be exercised by a
sufficient deputy or deputies seems to have guarded against the
worst evils of official incompetence. Though bishops, archdeacons,
and cathedral chapters were ready to appoint relatives or protégés
to offices of profit without regard to their suitability, both they and
the patentees realized that only with reliable deputies—painstaking
men like John Fardell, devoted to the drudgery of office—could the
complex ecclesiastical administration function and the profits accrue.
It was because of the provision for deputies that the courts had ruled
that a grant of a registrarship to an infant was good, notwithstanding

---

[1] In all except the offices of Chapter Clerk, *Auditor Causarum*, and Commissary.
These conclusions are based on a study of the patent books of the Dean and Chapter
of Lincoln for the period 1568-1804, D. & C. Bij.2.4; Bij.3.17; Bij.2.5; Bij.2.6;
Bij.2.13; Bij.2.14; Bij.2.12. On these patent books, *see Lincolnshire Archives Committee: Archivists' Report* 15 (1963-64), pp. 31-38.
[2] E. Gibson, *Codex Juris Ecclesiastici Anglicani* (2nd ed., Oxford, 1761), p. 986.
[3] E. Cardwell, *Synodalia* (1842), I, p. 409.

the infancy, when there was a clause *per se vel deputatum suum sufficientem*.[1]

By patents dated 30 December 1785 John Green of Buckden, notary public, and his son, Samuel Watkins Green, then aged four, were granted the two offices of registrar under the Bishop and his Commissary in the Archdeaconries of Lincoln and Stow, with all the fees, profits, and commodities of the offices, to be exercised 'by themselves or their sufficient deputy or deputies for whom they shall be answerable . . . for and during their natural lives and the life of the longer liver of them'.[2] These patents were granted by Bishop Thomas Thurlow, but the Greens owed the offices to the fact that John was the elder nephew of John Green, Bishop of Lincoln from 1761 to 1779. A bachelor himself, Bishop Green used his patronage to advance the children and grandchildren of his brother, who is said to have been a miller at Beverley.[3] In 1762 he had granted a patent of the office of Registrar under the Bishop's Commissary in the Archdeaconry of Leicester to the same John, described as of Beverley, gentleman, and to Robert Dowbiggin, clerk, husband of John's sister Elizabeth, to be held jointly for their lives and the life of the longer liver of them.[4] By 1766 John had moved to Buckden, when, described as Lieutenant, he was married there to Miss Sarah Dixson of Ramsey.[5] In 1769 Bishop Green appointed John and his infant son John to the Principal Registrarship of the diocese and the registrarships under the Bishop's Commissaries in the archdeaconries of Lincoln and Stow.[6] The registrarship under the Commissary of Leicester he now granted jointly to his second nephew, Thomas Green, then a Lieutenant in the 51st Regiment of Foot, and to Robert Dowbiggin, whom in this year he promoted to be a canon of Lincoln, prebendary of Welton Brinkhall and Subdean of Lincoln Cathedral.[7] Bishop Green had also used the bishopric estate to further his family's fortunes. While the Bishop lived, the leasehold property which John held from him he held only in name, in trust for his uncle's own benefit.[8] By his will of 1778, however, the Bishop

---

[1] *The Third Part of the Reports of Sir George Croke* (3rd impression, 1683), p. 556.

[2] Bij.2.12, pp. 256-60; Register 39, pp. 438-41.

[3] Sir Francis Hill, *Georgian Lincoln* (Cambridge, 1968), p. 35, quoting the Rev. William Cole.

[4] Bij.2.12, pp. 41-42.

[5] Buckden parish registers at Buckden Church, Register 11.

[6] Bij.2.12, pp. 87b-92; Reg. 39, pp. 117-21.
The cash payment for confirmation of these patents by the Dean and Chapter was £29 8s. 0d. (account of John Bradley with John Green, 1769-70 in Box 'Officials').

[7] Bij.2.12, pp. 93-94; Reg. 39, pp. 121-23. In 1794, on Dowbiggin's death, Thomas Green, described as late a Captain in the 41st Regiment of Foot but then of Ramsey, Hunts., received a new patent of this office from Bishop Pretyman, jointly with William Edward Pretyman, son of the Bishop (Bij.2.12, pp. 344-45). For Dowbiggin, *see Georgian Lincoln*, p. 36; J. A. Venn, *Alumni Cantabrigienses*, pt. II.

[8] In 1767 Bishop Green granted John a lease for twenty-one years of the rectory of Alford. The lease was renewed for the same term in 1777, but by his will the Bishop bequeathed this lease "taken in the name of my nephew John Green in trust for me" to Corpus Christi College, Cambridge. The college renewed it in 1784 (2 C.C. 34/97444, p. 240; 2 C.C. 35/97445, pp. 66, 166).

D

left John his leases of Harthay and of the little Vineyard in Buckden. In name John already held the two leases, granted in 1775, of the nether part of a meadow called the Nether Vineyard (3 acres) which lay at the back of the parsonage of Buckden and of parts of the meadows and pastures called Harthay in the parish of Brampton, Hunts., a total of 139 acres. The Bishop also left John his leasehold property at Over and his estate at Hail Weston, £800, £200 for each of his five children, the residue of his plate, and half the residue of the estate, which was divided between the two brothers, described now as Major John Green and Captain Thomas Green.[1]

Bishop Green died in 1779, but his grants of office to his relatives, duly confirmed by the Dean and Chapter, were good against his successors. In 1778 Major John Green's wife Sarah had died. He married his second wife, Margaret Watkins of Buckden, spinster, on 8th November 1780, and she was the mother of Samuel Watkins Green, born probably in 1781.[2] John, the eldest son by the first marriage, who had shared in his father's patents of 1769, died in 1785.[3] Major Green therefore surrendered his patents so that new ones could be granted. After negotiations with Bishop Thurlow about the lives to be included, new ones were drawn up and sent to Lincoln for confirmation by the Dean and Chapter.[4] Green secured the insertion of his son, Samuel Watkins Green, as the second life in the patents of registrarship under the Bishop's Commissary in the Archdeaconries of Lincoln and Stow, but the new life inserted in the patent of the principal registrarship was that of the Bishop's eldest son, Edward Thurlow, also an infant aged four.[5] John Green died in 1793,[6] and from this date the proceeds from the two patent offices were the sole property of Samuel Watkins Green, still a minor.[7] These

[1] Will dated 17 Aug. 1778, proved 11 May 1779, P.C.C., Somerset House; 2 C.C. 35/97445, pp. 37, 41. In 1768 the Bishop had granted two leases of these properties to his secretary, John Hodgson, in trust for himself, but Hodgson surrendered them in 1775 (2 C.C. 34/97444, pp. 256, 260). The leases of 1775 were granted for the lives of John Green, of his second son, Thomas, then aged six, and of Joseph Yorke, son of the then Dean of Lincoln and Bishop of St. David's. In 1792 John Green relinquished the Harthay properties, which were again leased to John Hodgson, but he renewed the lease of the 3 acres of the Nether Vineyard for the same three lives as in the lease of 1775 (2 C.C. 35/97445, pp. 326, 329).

[2] Buckden parish registers, 4 and 11. The baptism of Samuel Watkins Green is not recorded in the Buckden registers and the year of his birth has been calculated from a lease of 1799, in which he was said to be about eighteen (2 C.C. 71/92718), and from letter 16, p. 60 below.

[3] Buckden registers, 5.

[4] Surrender, dated 15 Dec. 1785, in box 'Officials'; Cor. R. 8/12, 13.

[5] Bj.2.12, pp. 253-55; Reg. 39, p. 437. John Green's life interest in the patent was secured by Bishop Thurlow giving him a bond that Edward should not interfere in the profits or appointment of deputies (Cor. R. 8/16, 19, 20). For Edward Thurlow, see G. E. C., Complete Peerage XII (1953), p. 732.

[6] Buckden registers, 6.

[7] Accounts of John Fardell as deputy to the Registrars of the Commissary and Archdeacon of Lincoln show that for the year 1792-3 the profits were paid to Dr. Dowbiggin as executor of John Green, and from 1793 onwards they were usually remitted to Mrs. Green, mother and guardian of S. W. Green. S. W. Green first signed in receipt of them on 3 October 1802 (R./Ac. 3/5 and 6).

offices were virtually his only provision, since his father left him little under his will of 1792: merely some plate, a clock, the reversion of a parcel of fen in Ramsey after his mother's death, a legacy of £5 at the age of twenty-one, a fifth share of any personal estate which might exist after the payment of all debts and legacies, and some silver and furniture, if his step brother Thomas Green failed to return to England from Africa within twenty years to claim them.[1] No references to Samuel Watkins Green have been found after the close of this correspondence in 1805. It is reasonable to infer that he died in 1819, as the next patents of the offices which he held were granted on 13th December in that year and related that the offices were vacant by his death.[2]

John Fardell, recipient of these letters, was Deputy Registrar at Lincoln from 1783 until his sudden death in 1805, twelve days after the last of these letters. From his boyhood he had worked in the office of John Bradley, Deputy Registrar: he is found there in 1760, when he was probably in his fifteenth year.[3] In 1767 he became one of the proctors in the Consistory Court and by 1774 was a notary public.[4] On Bradley's death in 1783, he succeeded him, and in the same year he married 'Nelly', Eleanor Penelope, daughter of John Hayward of Lincoln.[5] By his will Bradley gave to Fardell his messuage in Eastgate and also his cottages and orchard in Northgate, all leasehold of the Dean and Chapter, in trust that he should pay the rent, renew the term, and allow his widow to enjoy the property and to take the residue of the profits during her life. After her death he gave the remainder of the terms and the benefit of renewal absolutely to Fardell.[6] Fardell had been living in the Bail of Lincoln, but from 1784 is described as of the parish of St. Peter-in-Eastgate.[7] He was in occupation of the house in 1788, when he renewed the

[1] Will dated 31 May 1792, proved 10 June 1793, P.C.C., Somerset House. Most of John Green's landed property was bequeathed to his youngest son, John George Green, then an infant, and to his widow Margaret. The two surviving sons of the first marriage, Thomas Green and Charles Dixson Green, had already received legacies from Bishop Green and provision from their parents. Thomas was installed as a writer in the service of the Africa Company at Cape Coast Castle.

[2] Register 40, p. 300. No will has been found.

[3] D. & C. Bij.5.1, p. 396. According to J. Burke, *History of the Commoners of Great Britain and Ireland* (1838) IV, pp. 246-47, he was born in 1744 and his father died when he was an infant. But according to a lease of Bottesford parsonage, made on 29 September 1794, Fardell was then aged forty-eight, which makes 1746 the year of his birth (D. & C. Bij.5.6, f. 201). His parents William Fardell and Catherine Hubbert were married at St. Mary Magdalene's, Lincoln, on 21 September 1742 (*The Parish Registers of the City of Lincoln, Marriages* 1538-1754 (Lincoln Record Society Parish Register Section, IX), p. 76).

[4] Cj.41; D. & C. Bij.2.12, f. 134.

[5] Burke's *Commoners* IV, p. 246.

[6] Will, 31 Jan. 1783, proved 19 June, L.C.C. 1783. He also left Fardell his pew in St. Peter-in-Eastgate, all his law books, and such other books as he should choose out of Bradley's collections, with the exception of four works designated for the cathedral library. Bradley had received leases of the house for forty-year terms in 1760 and 1774 (D. & C. Div. 97.1, pp. 13, 55). R./Ac. 14/1-4 are Fardell's accounts as Bradley's executor.

[7] D. & C. Div. 94.4a; Bij.5.5, f. 169.

D*

forty-year lease by paying a fine of £10 for fourteen years which had lapsed. The house, now numbers 18 and 18½, was on the north side of Eastgate, abutting on the churchyard of St. Peter in Eastgate on the east, and having a piece of ground and a well at the back, taken from the orchard or paddock of the house on the west side.[1] The 'Register Office' where he worked and where most of the diocesan records were stored was near at hand, in the north gate-house of the Close, on the site of the present Priory Gate.[2]

The office described as 'Deputy Registrar' was a composite one and consisted of the exercise of a number of separate employments, most of them held as deputy, of which the deputy registrarships under the Bishop and his Commissary in the Archdeaconries of Lincoln and Stow were only two.[3] In fact Fardell was the key figure in the transaction of the church's legal business at Lincoln. He worked in close collaboration and was in constant communication with John Hodgson, an ecclesiastical lawyer who was the Bishop's legal secretary.[4] Hodgson spent his time in London or at Buckden, according to the Bishop's movements, and dealt with all those matters which immediately came before the Bishop and required his personal attention. On 24 December 1785 Hodgson asked Fardell whether they ought not to have new deputations from Mr. Green, on his surrendering the old and taking new patents as Principal Registrar and Registrar under the Commissaries of Lincoln and Stow.[5] On 26 January 1786 he wrote telling Fardell that the Bishop wished him to send up to town his last appointment from Green, and he should have another in proper form: 'but I apprehend it will not say anything about payment of fees to either patentee'.[6] Fardell was of opinion that in order to be legally valid his appointment from the Principal Registrars ought to be the deed of both Green and of the minor, Edward Thurlow. The Bishop consulted legal experts and finally decided that a deputation from Green alone would be sufficient, but he agreed that if the least doubt remained in Fardell's

---

[1] D. & C. Bij.5.5, f. 393; Div. 97.1, p. 98. He renewed the lease again in 1799 for £8 fine (D. & C. Bij.5.7, ff. 16v.-17v.; Div. 97.2, unpaginated).

[2] *Reports from the Select Committee appointed to inquire into the State of the Public Records of the Kingdom, etc.* (1800), pp. 314-15; E. Venables, *Walks through the Streets of Lincoln* (1888), p. 26. For Thomas Sympson's vivid description of the confusion he found in Bradley's office in 1752, *see Lincolnshire Notes and Queries* IX (1907), pp. 86-87.

[3] For a survey of the courts of the Lincoln diocese and the deputy registrarships held by Fardell's son's successor, Robert Swan, *see Returns of all Courts which exercise Ecclesiastical Jurisdiction and of all Courts which exercise Peculiar and Exempt Jurisdiction in England and Wales* (1828), pp. 252-55.

[4] For John Hodgson, *see Archivists' Report* 19, 1967-68, pp. 48-50, and Cor. R. 8 *passim*.

[5] Cor. R. 8/13. As Hodgson's patent from the Bishop was to transact all such businesses as should immediately come before the Bishop and to be Keeper of the records in the Register Office within the palace at Buckden, he thought this power should be excepted or somehow noticed in Fardell's deputation. Fardell's deputation from the Principal Registrars included this exception. (Cor. R. 8/19, 21.)

[6] Cor. R. 8/15.

mind, he should prepare and send a deed to be executed by both parties.[1] Drafts, in his own hand, of Fardell's two deputations have survived, that from the Principal Registrars from John Green and Edward Thurlow, that from the Registrars under the Commissaries of Lincoln and Stow from John Green and Samuel Watkins Green.[2] In both appointments it was stated that Fardell was to pay two-third parts of the clear profits to the patentees, and to keep one-third himself as he had hitherto done.[3]

Fardell also exercised the registrarships under the Archdeacons of Lincoln and Stow, the former as deputy, the latter by virtue of a patent grant of the registrarship. It was the practice within these two archdeaconries for the officials of the Bishop and of the Archdeacon to exercise a concurrent jurisdiction, and the fees for probate business and the granting of marriage licences were equally divided between the Commissaries of the Bishop and the Officials of the Archdeacons and their registrars. Thus in Fardell's accounts as deputy to the registrars of the Commissary and Archdeacon of Lincoln, each year half of the net profits were due to Green as registrar under the Commissary of Lincoln, minus one-third for acting, and plus the small sum which represented his receipts on the Stow account.[4]

Fardell himself held the office of registrar under the Archdeacon of Stow. In 1781 the Archdeacon, John Towne, had granted a patent of this office to John Bradley and to Fardell, to be held successively for term of their lives and for the life of the longer liver, on Bradley's surrender of a former patent to him and to the Archdeacon's son.[5] Fardell can have had little profit as he had to enter into a bond in £300 to Leonard Towne of Grantham, gentleman, which bound him, in case he survived Bradley, to pay £15 a year to Leonard during the lives of John and Benjamin Towne, sons of the Archdeacon

[1] Cor. R. 8/16, 19, 20, 100.
[2] Cor. R. 8/21, 22.
[3] The arrangement whereby the deputy received a third of the clear profits for acting seems to have been usual. In a return of annual emoluments of registrars in ecclesiastical courts based on an average of the years 1827-29, the Deputy Registrar in the Courts of the Commissary of the Bishop in the Archdeaconries of Lincoln and Stow and in the Archdeacon of Lincoln's court was still receiving one-third though the deputy to the Principal Registrar had two-fifths in 1827 and 1828 (*Reports of the Commissioners on the Practice and Jurisdiction of the Ecclesiastical Courts*, pp. 314, 556). In applying the Act 5 Edward VI c. 16 against buying and selling of offices, the Courts followed Lyndwood's dictum that anyone having spiritual jurisdiction might assign to a deputy a certain sum for his salary or a certain proportion of the gains, the deputy answering to him for the whole gain. It was not permissible for the deputy to pay the principal a fixed sum, and to retain the residue for his labour (Gibson, *op. cit.*, pp. 980-81).
[4] R./Ac. 3/2; *Archivists' Report* 19, pp. 47-48; R./Ac. 3/4, 5, 6. The other half of the profits, minus a third, was paid to the Archdeacon of Lincoln's registrar, plus receipts on a separate account for inductions and churchwardens' fees. In 1799 Archdeacon John Pretyman had granted the registrarship in Lincoln Archdeaconry to the Rev. Charles Gordon and to his own son John Pretyman (D. & C. Bij.2.12, pp. 399-402). Gordon died in 1802.
[5] Bij.2.12, ff. 203-05.

so long as he should exercise the office. In 1788, at the request of Mr. Towne, Fardell substituted a bond in the same sum to Anne and Margaret Towne of Henrietta Street, Covent Garden, 'dealers in child bedlinen' for the payment to them of £15 a year during the life of the same Benjamin Towne.[1] In 1801 Fardell obtained a new patent, jointly with his eldest son John, for their lives and the life of the longer liver of them.[2]

In 1783 Fardell had also succeeded Bradley as deputy to Anthony Reynolds, who had been granted the office of Chapter Clerk for life in 1757, to be exercised by himself or his deputy or deputies approved by the Dean and Chapter. Fardell received the usual one-third of the profits.[3]

Fardell's remuneration as a deputy was modest. In his evidence to the Commissioners on the practice and jurisdiction of the ecclesiastical courts in 1830, the Archdeacon of Lincoln deplored the fact that his registrar's office should be performed by deputy: 'it is an office that would be sufficiently paid if the principal did his own duty; but it must be very insufficiently paid when the principal takes the larger part of the stipend and gives only a small portion to the party that performs the office'.[4] In 1803 Fardell estimated the annual profit to the patentee from the registrarship under the Commissaries of Lincoln and Stow at about £140 or £150 a year, after a deduction of a third for transacting the business, and other estimates and the actual receipts recorded in the accounts accord with this figure.[5] The deputy's remuneration was therefore only £70 to £75. In fact the tenure of many offices by the deputy partly solved this difficulty.

One office led to another, and a painstaking notary with an office

[1] D. & C. Div. 94.4a.

[2] Bij.2.12, ff. 424-25; Reg. 40, p. 27.

[3] Bij.2.14, ff. 347-49, patent to A. Reynolds. D. & C. Div. 97.3 is Bradley's account book as deputy to Reynolds as Chapter Clerk, 1773-83. One-third of the net profits were paid to Bradley for acting. His third ranged in value from £10 3s. 3d. to £56 11s. 1d. a year. Anthony Reynolds was a grandson of Bishop Reynolds of Lincoln, and son of George Reynolds, Chancellor of Peterborough and Archdeacon and Subdean of Lincoln (J. & J. A. Venn, *Alumni Cantabrigienses*, pt. I; A. R. Maddison, *Lincolnshire Pedigrees* (Harleian Soc. LII, 1904), p. 819).

[4] *Reports of the Commissioners on the Practice and Jurisdiction of the Ecclesiastical Courts* . . . (1832), p. 138.

[5] Letters 9 and 13 pp. 57 and 59 below. To the bishop, however, Fardell put the average annual profit at £130 (letter 16, p. 60 below). In 1785 this joint registrarship was said to be worth upon an average of ten years last past £133 8s. 7d. (Spec. 2, p. 365). By another estimate (Spec. 7, p. 405) the registrarship under the Commissary of Lincoln was worth £133 8s. 7d. on an average of eight years ending in 1782, and the registrarship under the Commissary of Stow £13 5s. 3d. on an average for the same period. In 1809, in a declaration for property-tax purposes, John Fardell junior declared that the annual account of fees he received to the use of Samuel Watkins Green amounted to £150 (D. & C. Cii.78.1). The annual average for the three years 1827-29 was £160 13s. 0d. (*Returns of all Courts which exercise Ecclesiastical Jurisdiction and of all Courts which exercise Peculiar and Exempt Jurisdiction . . .* p. 556). The actual receipts recorded in the deputy's account books show that in the period 1793-1805 the patentee's two-thirds might be as high as £194 or under £110 (R./Ac. 3/5 and 6).

near the Cathedral could add to his official appointments and secure his own and his family's advancement. Pluralism not only enabled the deputy to prosper, but also served a useful purpose in centralizing ecclesiastical administration in a few hands. A lifetime of unremitting labour in the registry office, combined with the multiplicity of his offices, equipped Fardell to deal with every conceivable legal matter relating to diocese and cathedral. In 1793 the Dean and Chapter appointed him Clerk of the Fabric, Clerk of the Common Chamber and Receiver General, Coroner within their liberties, and Steward of the Galilee Court within the Close and of six of their manor courts.[1] It was probably at this time that he became Receiver to the Bishop of Lincoln. As early as 1786 Hodgson had advised him that there was no impropriety in his applying to the Bishop for the office in case of the demise of William Jepson, the ailing holder.[2] It is not clear from this correspondence why Fardell failed to secure the insertion of his son's life into the patents of registrarship in place of Green's in 1803.

Fardell's position enabled him to lease and to purchase church lands. In Lincoln, in addition to his dwelling house next to St. Peter's, he acquired other leasehold property from the Dean and Chapter. In 1784 he was granted a forty-year lease of a tenement in the parish of St. Paul in the Bail, and he renewed a lease for forty years of a tenement and stable lately erected with a piece of ground belonging in Northgate, in the parish of St. Peter-in-Eastgate, which had been granted to Bradley in 1768.[3] In 1785 he acquired a lease for forty years of the house in Eastgate adjoining his dwelling house, with the orchard to the west of the house, together with two arable lands in the open fields.[4] Apart from his dwelling house and stable, the property was sub-let. He also owned freehold property in the Bail of Lincoln[5].

Fardell was also able to invest in freehold and leasehold property outside Lincoln. By 1790 he owned land at Welton by Lincoln, and by 1800 had freehold estate at Thorpe on the Hill.[6] In 1792, for a fine of £1260 he acquired from the Dean and Chapter a lease for

[1] D. & C. Bij.2.12, ff. 335-38. These offices were granted during pleasure only.
[2] Cor. R. 8/23. 'The office is trifling in point of profit, being only £13.6.8. p.ann., besides fees on admission of a few copyhold tenants and the use of cash in hand, as it is customary to make up the annual Lady Day account the Xtmas following and the rents are or should be paid soon after due.' see also Cor. R. 8/84, 87, 91. Fardell held other minor employments, e.g., as receiver and registrar for the Prebendary of Bishop Norton (Cor. R. 5/23), receiver for the Prebendaries of Corringham and Stow (R./Ac. 14/6), and in a purely secular capacity as attorney for Hugh Castleman, a pilot at Calcutta, to manage his affairs in Lincoln including property in the Bail (R./Ac. 14/5; D. & C. Aiv.10.84).
[3] D. & C. Bij.5.5, ff. 165v., 169; D. & C. Div.97.1, p. 84.
[4] Bij.5.5, f. 224. He paid £20 fine (Div. 97.1, p. 89). He renewed the lease in 1799 for £20 (D. & C. Bij.5.7, f. 14; Div. 97.2, unpaginated). Here Fardell's widow lived after his death. She died in 1824 (L.C.C. wills, 1824, administration with will annexed).
[5] Will of John Fardell, 3 June 1800, proved 2 April 1805. P.C.C. Somerset House.
[6] Lindsey Q.S.: Land Tax, Lawress; Fardell's will.

three lives of Bottesford parsonage, Lincolnshire, a property valued at £306 a year net in 1799.[1] In 1800 he bought the freehold of the parsonage for £2,482 19s. 6d. under the Acts of 38 and 39 George III empowering the sales of the reversions of church estates for raising money for the redemption of land tax.[2] He was himself acting as agent of the Dean and Chapter in the redemption of the tax on their estates.[3] In 1795, for £84 fine he acquired from the Dean and Chapter a lease for twenty-one years of 34 acres of pasture ground in South Somercotes.[4] In the same year, for £2,100 he secured an assignment of a lease of the prebend of Stow for the remainder of a term of three lives granted in 1759. Six weeks later, in 1796, on surrendering this lease and paying £100, he received a new lease from the prebendary which included Fardell's son Thomas, aged four, as the third life.[5]

When Fardell died suddenly on 16 February 1805 he was succeeded in his offices by his eldest son John, a barrister-at-law, who had already been doing some work at the registry.[6] He also succeeded his father in the house next to St. Peter's and bought its freehold from the Dean and Chapter in 1810.[7] In this year, on the death of Anthony Reynolds, he became Chapter Clerk in name.[8] While aged only thirty-seven, he retired from office. By a deed of covenant dated 26th March 1821, for the sum of £7,000 he sold and assigned over to Robert Swan his business as a proctor at Lincoln and the divers other employments which he had exercised.[9] This sum may have been later invested in his purchase of a country estate. By 1833 he was lord of the manor of Greetham and possessor of estates in that lordship and in the hamlet of Holbeck in the parish of Ashby Puerorum. A plan of his estate includes elevations of his residence, Holbeck

[1] C.C. 4/150085; D. & C. Div. 97.2, unpaginated; valuation, C.C. 4/152762. The lease of 1792 was for the lives of Michael Morley Bacon Morley of Kirton, gent., of John Fardell, the lessee's son, and of Catherine, his daughter. In 1794, for a fine of £154:1:5, he secured the insertion of his own life in place of Morley's.

[2] D. & C. Bij.2.12, ff. 412-18. Seeking the advice of Mr. Renshaw, surveyor, on 22 May 1799 Fardell confessed himself very doubtful about purchasing his own lease, as he supposed not less than £2500 would be expected. 'I think I should not consult the interest of my family by giving so much, as £1000 invested in the Funds will afford an ample provision for renewals, supposing one to take place every twelve years.' (D. & C. Cii.78.1).

[3] D. & C. Civ.95.3.

[4] D. & C. Bij.5.6, f. 248v.; Div.97.2. He renewed the lease in 1802 and paid £27.6s.6d. fine for it (ibid.).

[5] C.C. 131/97400, 97402, 97403.

[6] *Lincoln, Rutland and Stamford Mercury*, 22 Feb. 1805. He was buried on 21 February (Bishop's Transcripts, St. Peter-in-Eastgate, Lincoln).

[7] D. & C. Patent Register 1805-56, pp. 38-43. By his will Fardell left all his lands, tenements, tithes, and freehold estate to his three sons, John, Thomas, and Henry, as tenants in common, charged with an annuity of £200 to his widow.

[8] *ibid.*, pp. 36-37.

[9] D. & C. Chapter Clerk, Parcel 36.

House, an unpretentious house in the classical style.[1] He became a magistrate and Deputy Lieutenant and represented Lincoln in the Parliament of 1830-31.[2]

It seems appropriate that many of the descendants of John Fardell the elder were Anglican clergy. His younger sons, Thomas and Henry, were educated at Cambridge and ordained. Thomas, an LL.D., was rector of Boothby Pagnell 1831-46 and of Sutton, Cambridgeshire, 1846-51. Henry was a canon of Ely and married the eldest daughter of the Bishop of Ely, whose chaplain he became. Incumbent of several parishes in Cambridgeshire and Norfolk, he was a Justice of the Peace for the Isle of Ely and for Norfolk and Lincolnshire and Chairman of Quarter Sessions. Fardell's two daughters, each of whom received £2,500 under his will, and a further £500 on their mother's death, were married to Lincolnshire incumbents.[3] John Fardell the younger has been called 'a pleasant nonentity',[4] a description which may fittingly be applied to the whole family which achieved modest success but no great prominence. Yet it was precisely because John Fardell the elder had been a nonentity, willing to be immersed for life in the drudgery of office, that the cumbrous administration of the unreformed church could function.

---

[1] Plan of 1833, Misc. Dep. 102/1. Purchase deeds of only part of this property have been found. In 1829, for £17,000, he bought four farms and several closes and the Black Horse Inn, all in Greetham, totalling 567a. 28p. At the same time, for £760, he acquired the lordship, graveship, and bailiwick of Greetham, a brick kiln, six cottages, and 24a. 2r. 26p. in several parcels, lately held as copyhold of the manor of Greetham (B.R.A. 1622/1/1/16-27). Sale particulars of 1828 of freehold estates totalling nearly 2,300a. which include this Greetham property show that the lordships of Ashby Puerorum and Holbeck were offered for sale at the same time (Padley 3/93). On Fardell's purchases, see also Dixon 19/1/11. Opinions differ as to whether Fardell completely built Holbeck House, in place of an old farmhouse, or whether he merely added to a house built in 1823. The house, however, does not appear in the sale particulars of 1828. The romantic landscaping seems to have been his work (J. Conway Walter, Records Historical and Antiquarian of Parishes round Horncastle (Horncastle, 1904), pp. 11-12; N. Pevsner and J. Harris, The Buildings of England: Lincolnshire (1964), p. 173).
[2] Burke, op. cit., p. 246. For his parliamentary candidature and opposition to the Reform Bill, see Hill, op. cit., pp. 233-234.
[3] For John Fardell's children and descendants, see Dixon 15/2/45; Burke, op. cit., pp. 246-47; J. A. Venn, Alumni Cantabrigienses, pt. II (1940-54); Joseph Foster, Men at the Bar (1885); Sir Bernard Burke, Peerage, Baronetage and Knightage (1913). Catherine Fardell was married to Henry Bassett, vicar of Glentworth and rector of North Thoresby, 1802-52, and vicar of Saxby 1805-52 (Reg. 40, pp. 40, 96, 534, 535, 537). Mary Fardell was wife of George Moore, perpetual curate of St. Peter-in-Eastgate with St. Margaret, Lincoln, 1820-41, and rector of Owmby 1823-41.
[4] Hill, op. cit., p. 233.

LETTERS

1. *Samuel Watkins Green of St Neots to John Fardell at Lincoln*
Huntingdon, 28 November 1802.

I came to this place this morning to meet Mr Flowers[1] whose attempts to procure me the money I wanted has proved quite ineffectual, and I am at length compelled to have recourse to your goodness in endeavouring to comply with what I purpose him setting forth. As I cannot sufficiently explain to any persons in this neighbourhood the kind of security I am able to offer, and at the same time I do not wish it to be known what the value of my office is, I have to beg you will do me the favor to advance it by degrees: that is the sum of three hundred pounds in about a fortnight from this day, and the remaining two hundred the first week in January, making in the whole the sum of £500. I would much rather you would advance me the money in this way than apply any longer to any one else, as I cannot, I am fearful, procure it unless you will favor me. I will secure the repayment to you by a bond and charge as a further security the annual produce of my office, and I hope and trust I shall be able to return it, the whole money again, in about a year and a half. I have been furnishing a house which I have taken at St Neots and am in immediate wants of money, and as I can get a draft upon you at 14 days cashed, I hope you will excuse my so doing. I am so much at this time put to it for cash that I really am driven to do what you perhaps may not altogether approve of, that is drawing upon you before I get your leave, but I hope you will see the necessity in proper light and not think I am imposing upon your goodness; far from it, I have every reason to be under particular obligations for repeated civilities and should feel most severely your bad opinion. At this period of my life I stand really in need of pecuniary aid, and I trust the method I have proposed will meet your goodness; and that done, I shall feel myself completely happy and think myself capable of withstanding any future change of Fortune. I will send you a bond for the whole sum immediately I get the draft upon you for £300 cashed, and will do any thing else you may require for a further security. I am, dear sir, yours most respectfully.

Endorsement: 28 Nov. 1802. Mr Green informing me he has drawn upon me for £300, with answer that I shall not accept his draft.

[1] William Flowers of Ramsey, attorney at law, seems to have been the family lawyer of the Greens. He was witness of the will of John Green of Buckden in 1792, and made an affidavit in 1793 that he had made the will, had had it copied, and had made various alterations in it before its execution (P.C.C., Somerset House).

2. *John Fardell to Samuel Watkins Green*
Lincoln, 2 December 1802, Thursday afternoon.

I presume you had not received my letter of the 29th ultimo when you wrote your letter on Monday. If you had, you would not have sent your servant, as that letter is in fact an answer to it. I can only add thereto that it is impossible to procure money here unless a proper and ample security is offered for it. No one will advance money upon the security of your office unless your life is insured and it is done by way of granting an annuity—which will be a most expensive mode of raising money and what as a friend I would not advise you to do, if it be possible to avoid it. I cannot in justice to my own family advance any money without a proper security for it. I am, dear sir, your obedient servant.

Endorsement: Answer to Mr Green's letter of 29 Nov. 1802.

3. *Samuel Watkins Green to John Fardell*
St Neots, 13 December 1802.
I should [*torn*] myself greatly obliged if you will hav[e the] kindness to direct me a draft at 14 days for £70 in . . . . executors of the late Mr B . . . for the furniture I purchased in the house I am going to live in at a public sale the other day. This is the only sum at present I stand in need of and I hope you will not scruple advancing it: as I have purchased them, I shall feel extremely hurt at not being able to pay for them. Your answer by return of post will oblige y[*torn*]s most respectfully.

3a. *Draft of Fardell's reply endorsed*
14 December 1802.
It is not in my power [to] comply with your request. I cannot do it and preserve my own credit. The sums necessary for the conduct of my own business are larger than you may suppose. I shall be ready to pay money when it is due, but I cannot do it before. I am, dear sir, your most obedient servant.

4. *John Fardell to Samuel Watkins Green*
Lincoln, 1 January 1803.
I always have been and still am ready to render you any service in my power consistent with the prior obligations I owe to my own family, but it cannot be expected that I can enter into engagements for the payment of money, or advance it without a proper security and indemnity. I must ingenuously inform you it will be impossible to raise money upon the security of your office, unless by the ruinous mode of annuity which it would be very imprudent to adopt. If your mother[1] and Mr Hodgson[2] can devise any means by which I can serve you without hazarding the injury of my own family, I shall be ready to do it, but I cannot in justice to them do otherwise.

[1] Margaret Green (née Watkins) was left a widow with three young children on John Green's death in 1793. See introduction, p. 44 above.
[2] For John Hodgson of London and Buckden, Secretary to the Bishop of Lincoln, see introduction, p. 46 above.

5. *Samuel Watkins Green to John Fardell*

St Neots, 6 January 1803.

I have duly received yours in answer to my last, for which I thank you. Since I last wrote to you I have had some conversation with an intimate friend of ours, Mr Maule of Huntingdon,[1] upon the subject of raising the money; and he thought the wisest way for me to do was (if I was upon terms sufficiently intimate with you to make the request) to beg you if practicable to advance the sum wanted, taking my bond for securing due payment of the principal and interest. I told him I had taken the liberty to make the request to you, and that you seemed to think that security not sufficiently strong. He then said secure your life: I should conceive that sufficiently secure. This was his opinion and it was also the opinion of two other friends [to] whom I mentioned the subject, as being the pleasantest way between all parties. If, therefore, you will agree and will oblige me by taking this security, you will enable me to set forward in my profession in life with safety and pleasure and confer a lasting favor on me. But should you not think well to favor me, I must then most certainly have recourse to the method of granting an annuity. You are the only friend I have that I can apply to for that I now want: those nearest allied have it not to advance me; and had not my good friend Mr Hodgson the highest opinion of your goodness and disposition towards me to render me all the service in your power, I should not have thus presumed to trouble you upon this subject. If in either of these cases you think my attendance again necessary at Lincoln, I shall with pleasure attend upon you. I must beg leave to urge your early answer, as on the 20th of this month I go to London for my admittance and the money I shall necessarily want ere that time arrives or I cannot be admitted, nor shall be able to do anything and must in consequence be miserable beyond description. Hoping to receive your favourable attention to this, I remain dear sir, yours respectfully.

[1] George Frederick Maule appears in *Clarke's New Law List* (1817, p. 141) as a country attorney at Huntingdon.

6. *John Fardell to Samuel Watkins Green*

Lincoln, 8 January 1803.

I am sorry that you should have troubled yourself to apply to me again upon the subject of advancing you money, as I thought I had fully expressed to you my situation and inability to comply with your request. I have hitherto avoided involving either myself or family in pecuniary difficulties and it is my determination if possible to adhere to the same mode of practice. I cannot in justice to my family advance money or become responsible for it upon such a security as you propose, and I am sure Mr Hodgson would not recommend any such thing to me.

Any thing that Mr Hodgson might think right and proper for me to do, I would to the best of my ability comply with, but rather than involve my family in difficulties and disputes I would quit the office. Your coming here can be of no use. If Mr Hodgson should think of any thing that might be useful to you and will write to me upon the subject, I will certainly give every attention in my power to it.

7.   Samuel Watkins Green to John Fardell

Eynesbury, near St Neots, 23 February 1803.

If perfectly convenient I should feel myself obliged by your remittance of £15 between this and Saturday. I have the pleasure to inform you of my having been admitted in the Court of King's Bench and inrolled in Chancery as a solicitor, and in case you have any business in these parts that I can dispatch, I should feel a pleasure in doing it. I am dear sir, yours respectfully.

Endorsement: Feb. 23rd. Mr Green for £15. Sent him same 25th Feb. 1803.

8.   William Abbott to John Fardell

St Neots, 11 April 1803.

I hope you will excuse the liberty of a stranger in addressing you on the following business.

Mr Green, attorney in Eynesbury, has had some considerable concerns in the money buisness, such as drawing bills on London which are not accepted. The reason he assigns is that he has not been able to obtain a certain security from Lincoln. The question I wish to ask you is, if that is the truth, as you know of, and wither it is ever likely to be as Mr Green affirms it is. Now above a fortnight since he gave me to understand it would arrive in London, so as to enable him to take up his draft, and it has not yet arrived. Sir, if you will have the goodness to say by return of post when it will or wither it is ever likely, you will much oblige yours &c.

Direct to William Abbott, upholsterer, St Neots, Hunts.

8a.   Draft of Fardell's reply endorsed

Lincoln, 12 April 1803.

By your addressing me respecting a security being sent to Mr Green, I presume my name has been made use of to you. [*torn*] shall be glad to know in what manner and [*torn*]ly to observe to you that Mr Green has an office here the fees of which to the present time have been remitted to him, and that he will always receive them as soon as they are due, so long as they shall pass through my hands. I am, dear sir, your obedient servant.

9. *John Fardell to William Abbott*

Lincoln, 26 July 1803.

The profits of Mr Green's office arises from the fees received for probates of wills, grants of administration, and marriage licences, the number of which being uncertain, the emoluments must of course vary every year. As near as I can form an opinion, I think the profits average about £140 or 50 per annum after a deduction of one-third for transacting the business,—but once in three years when the Bishop visits there is a suspension of the jurisdiction for three months, and during that period the fees are paid to the Bishop's Register[1]. That is the case in this present year, and as Mr Green has drawn upon me for more than was due to him at Lady day, I shall have very little in hand till after the Michaelmas Visitation, the latter end of October, when I shall receive the fees for the licences, and after that time shall be ready to account and pay the balance in hand and regularly remit it half yearly as it becomes due.

I have received a letter from Mr Green to pay the profits of his office into your hands, but you should send me a copy of the deed by which he has transferred it to you that I may be fully authorised to pay the money into your hands and judge whether I can with propriety answer any drafts of Mr Green's.

I shall be ready to give you every information in my power if you and Mr Green think proper to come here, but I cannot say that at present I think there is any necessity for your taking the journey. My stay at Buckden was only a few hours on Sunday the 10th instant, and as I had not the pleasure of seeing you on the 27th of May, I concluded you had received all the information you wished for. Mr Reynolds of Paxton[2], Mr Hodgson of Buckden, or Mr Watson of Huntingdon[3] will be able to give you an account of the office and how the business is transacted.

Mr Abbott, Upholder,
St Neots,
Huntingdonshire.

[1] On the profits of Green's office, see introduction, p. 48 above.
[2] Either Richard Reynolds of Little Paxton (d. 1814), son of the Rev. George Reynolds, Chancellor of Peterborough and Archdeacon and Subdean of Lincoln, who was High Sheriff of Cambridgeshire and Huntingdonshire 1776-77, or his nephew Lawrence, of Paxton Hall (d. 1839), son of the Rev. Anthony Reynolds, canon of Lincoln and Chapter Clerk, who was High Sheriff of Cambridgeshire and Huntingdonshire 1806-07 (Venn, *op. cit.*).
[3] Probably a surrogate. In 1786 'poor Watson of Huntingdon', a surrogate, was reported to be so bewildered that he must either be removed or the office would be ruined. He could not be prevailed upon to make accounts or to resign in favour of his sons (Cor. R. 8/42).

10. *William Abbott to John Fardell*

St Neots, 2 September 1803.

Your obliging letter of the 26th of July is now before me.

It is rendered necessary that you should give me the particular account of what money is in your hands, as I observe by your letter Mr Green has drawn on you for more money than was his due at the 25th of March last past. As it was agreed between Mr Green and myself that the profits should commence mine on the 25th of March last, subject to a certain obligation on me to pay the surplus into his hands, I must know what it is. Therefore I have no doubt but you will see it necessary (in order to adjust our accounts) that I should know what he has over drawn, as I may know how to apply the surpluss due to him. Your compliance with the request I now make (to send by the return of post an account of the monies in or out of your hands on the 25th of last March) you will much oblige, dear sir, your humble servant.

N.B. The copy of the deed of assignment shall be sent to you, if the order you have already received from Mr Green is not sufficient to authorise you to remitt the accounts and money (when due) to me, or any other authority you may wish for Mr Green will give you, for the time he may want it. As Mr Green is in want of a small sum in addition, must press an answer from you as soon as you conveniently can.

Endorsement: Answered 3d Sep. 1803.

11.   *John Fardell to William Abbott at St Neots*
3 September 1803.   On the 25th of March last Mr Green had received from me £86, and ten pounds more in April, which was considerably more than was then due to him; but the precise sum that was then due it is impossible for me to state 'till I receive the accounts from the Surrogates at the next Visitation. At present I am a considerable sum of money in advance, which will not be repaid me 'till the Visitation, when it is usual for the Surrogates to make a return of the licences they have dispatched and pay the money. I presume that the year's account to Michaelmas will not amount to £140: but I cannot say what the sum will be—it may be more or less—and Mr Green has had £106 from me. This is the best account I can give you 'till I get the returns from the Surrogates.

I have no doubt of your being lawfully authorized to receive the money, and am ready to pay it when I get it, but I should regularly ha[ve] a copy of the deed.

12.   *Samuel Watkins Green to John Fardell*
St Neots, 16 October 1803.
Will you have the goodness as soon as you possibly can to transmit Mr Abbott an account of the profits received in my office since September 1802 to September 1803. I am, dear sir, your respectful and obedient servant.

13. *John Fardell to William Abbott*

Lincoln, 20 October 1803.

When your letter of the 11th inst. arrived here I was just set out upon the Visitations round a part of this county which usually begin about the middle of October (never in September, as they cannot be before Michaelmas). I am only just returned home for three or four days and have to go the remaining part of the Visitation next week, after which I will immediately make up the year's account and pay the balance due. I have endeavoured to ascertain as near as I can what will be the profits of this year and [*torn*] weeks, and as I find there have been more licences made use of and business transacted than usual, it will exceed the sum I expected, and I have little doubt but it will amount to £150 or perhaps a little more. The particular sum I cannot ascertain 'till after next week, when the Visitations will be over.

I send you enclosed a draft for £30, and shall be glad to see you at Lincoln and shew you the accounts and pay the balance due any time after next week. Mr Green has had upon account one hundred and six pound.

There is no probability of my coming into Huntingdonshire. I have no calls there except at the Bishop's Visitation which is once in three years and was this year. Any information I can give you respecting the nature of the office I shall be ready to communicate to you, and am sir, your most obedient servant.

I beg my compliments to Mr Green.

14. *William Abbott to John Fardell*

St Neots, 22 October 1803.

Yours came to hand duly this morning incloseing a draft for thirty pounds at 14 days sight, for which accept of thanks. I will do myself the pleasure to see you at Lincoln as soon after the 3rd of Novembre as the nature of my buisness will admit, and remain, dear sir, your most obliged servant.

15. *Samuel Watkins Green to John Fardell*

Eynesbury, 20 November 1803.

I have been for some time past in treaty with Mr Abbott for the sale my patent places and he has at length determined upon the refusal of purchase, and as it is requisite for my own comfort and peace to obtain some money for the purpose of improving my situation and establishment, I have now to offer you the places for sale. If you can be satisfied with the insurance for my life, I am certain you will give for the purchase what in your mind you may deem fair and reasonable price, and I shall not doubt your judgment.

Will you therefore do me the favor to inform me what you will give provided the insurance meets your satisfaction. I am dear sir, your respectful and obedient servant.

P.S. I have not at this moment any cash to go on with and you will render me infinite service by advancing me £20.

Endorsement: 20 Nov. 1803. Mr Green offering his patent to me, with letter to the Bishop and his lordship answer.

16. *John Fardell to [George Pretyman] Bishop of Lincoln*
Lincoln, 22 November 1803.

My Lord, Mr Rutter communicated your Lordship's sentiments respecting the renewal of Tetney lease to the persons interested, and I have this day been desired by them to inform your Lordship they will be ready to pay the fine of £1584 12s. 2d. as soon as the leases can be prepared, for which purpose instructions are sent herewith in a separate paper. The parties could not be certain of the money being ready till now, otherwise they would have given an earlier answer to your Lordship's letter.[1]

I beg leave now to trouble your Lordship with a business which concerns myself and family. I have just received the inclosed letter from Mr Green. This proposal Mr Green has made to me might eventually be an object of importance to me, but I certainly shall not do anything in the business without your Lordship's concurrence and approbation. The average of the profits of the office is as near as may be about £130 per annum. At my time of life it would not be adviseable to advance a large sum of money for the purchase of Mr Green's life estate in the patent, as that would be no permanent settlement for my son; but if your Lordship would have the goodness to permit my son's life to be inserted in the patent instead of Mr Green's, I should have no objection to give him the fair value of his life interest in it for a surrender of his patent, if it could be properly and legally done. I have no pretensions to ask so great a favor of your Lordship, but having upon many occasions experienced your kindness and benevolence, and feeling it my duty as a parent to endeavour to promote the interest of my son, I am encouraged to solicit your Lordship's permission to substitute my son's life in the patent instead of Mr Green's. They are nearly of the same age, one 19 the other 22. If I am favoured by your Lordship, I will endeavour to agree with Mr Green; but if the business should not meet with your Lordship's approbation, I shall give up the idea, and request your Lordship to pardon the trouble I have given you.[2]

---

[1] By his will of 19 July 1802, proved 4 Feb. 1803 (L.C.C. 1803), the Rev. Thomas Howson bequeathed his property at Tetney to Henry Rutter of the City of Lincoln, esq., John Fardell, and the Rev. Charles Holland of Barkwith, whom he appointed as executors, in trust that they should sell it and apply the proceeds as directed. On 7 December 1803 the Bishop granted a lease to these three of the manor or chief mansion house called Cannon Garth in Tetney and the rectory of Tetney for three

lives, in trust for the uses expressed in Howson's will (2 C.C. 35/97446, p. 24). The property had been leased to Howson, then vicar of Langton, for three lives in 1773 (2 C.C. 34/97444, p. 346).

² The Bishop's reply to this letter has not been preserved, nor has Fardell's draft to Green reporting on it.

17. *John Fardell to Samuel Watkins Green at Eynesbury near St Neots*

Lincoln, 22 November 1803.

I am favoured with your letter and should have no objection to make a proper and reasonable compensation to you for your office, provided it can be done legally and with propriety, and the Bishop of Lincoln will consent to it, without whose concurrence I would not proceed in the business. I apprehend as matters are circumstanced the Insurance Offices would not insure your or any other young man's life likely to be called out into service in case of the Invasion without a very high premium, if at all; and before any proper estimate can be made of the value of the office it must be known upon what terms the insurance of your life could be made and whether they will insure against the chance of your being called into actual service, or going abroad. Another consideration is to be attended to which is that if the invasion takes place the business of the office will be at a stand and little or nothing done in it—and of course the profits be diminished. If the Bishop should assent to your transfer of the patent, I would much rather the compensation to be made to you should be estimated and named by any other person than myself. You probably are informed of or have estimated the value of it, but it cannot under the circumstances that attend it be considered as an annuity—the responsibility and hazard that attends it is more than you may be aware of—; however, with the Bishop's permission, I should have no objection to doing what was right and proper.

I am already so much money in advance for stamps and on account of the office that I must be excused advancing any more.

18. *Samuel Watkins Green to John Fardell*

St Neots, 25 December 1803.

Since I last wrote to you an unfortunate circumstance has happened to my friend Mr Abbott, who had a considerable sum of money in the hands of Messrs Perkins, the Bankers at Huntingdon, who have within this fortnight past become insolvent—and the confusion it has caused in this county is astonishing. What makes Mr Abbott's case the most distressing is that the money in their hands was the amount of the goods at the sale of the late Sir John Payne, and it was placed in Perkins' hands by Abbott as the place of greatest security; and now the executors of Sir J. Payne insist upon the money being immediately paid and as the amount is nearly a thousand pounds of course Mr A. finds great difficulty to settle it or whether he will be able is a great doubt. At the time this happened, he had agreed to advance me more money upon having the whole of the fees of my office assigned to him, and in consequence I am now reduced to the greatest distress. In the assignment he has of mine there is a special covenant to enable me to pay in the money advanced on giving 6 months' notice, and so on either side, and therefore his— Mr Abbott's—creditors cannot come unexpectedly upon me; and as he was so good as to serve me at a former period, I should wish if possible to serve him now. I have therefore a proposal to make to you which is: that if you can within 6 months repay the money advanced by him to me, together with the sum of £600 more (making in the whole £1200) within twelve months, upon having the security and insurance upon my life assigned over to you—the manner in which I should require my money to be paid to me would be to suffer me to draw upon you after date not less than a month at a time: this I presume may be more convenient to you and answering purpose of mine—and as at this time I am in great want of money to defray my house expences &c, a draft from you a month after date for any sum most convenient will be esteemed a favor. I should not thus press you for a remittance on account were I not on the eve of changing my situation in life, and consequently a small sum of money will be requisite. If you can conveniently accommodate me with a draft at 3 months after date for £200 (should you accept the assignment) on account, I can get it discounted and it would be of the greatest consequence to me. Should you not agree to accept the assignment, perhaps you may know of some persons with you who will, and I should feel obliged by your making the inquiry. As the time above-mentioned presses, I must request your answer with a small remittance by Thursday next—waiting your reply. I am, dear sir, yours truly obliged and respectfully.

Endorsement, in hand of Fardell: John Thomas Brown.

19. *William Abbott to John Fardell*

St Neots.

Mr Green came to me saying that he and you had agreed for a further mortgage on his two patent offices and that I might draw on you for the surplus over and above what reimbursed me, what I have already advanced, but said at the same time you could only permit me to draw for 20 pounds. I cannot understand what this can mean unless it was to get 20 pounds more out of me.

He (Mr G.) also informs me that you will take the whole profits of the offices upon yourself and are willing to pay a valuable consideration for them, and that you only wait for a satisfaction from the Insurance Office respecting the risks of his life. I have wrote to the Assurance Office respecting his present volenteer military engagements, and their answer is that they require no advance on the premium for volenteer services, even if there should be an invasion.

The Office would not say what they would require in case he went into the regular army, or into the East or West Indias; that must remain unknown untill he actually is gone into the regulars or to the East or West Indias.

Mr Green was married on Monday last, the 2nd of January 1804, to a young lady of small fortune, it is said about 600 pounds only expectant on the death of an old maiden aunt.[1]

I also understand from Mr G. that he has offered you his places for 1200 pounds. If you should accept his proposals and agree with him, will thank you to let me know that I may be present at the time and place where he receives the money. Have the goodness to tell me if any such thing is on foot, and also (if you can make up your mind) what you would give for the whole profits to take them (as he intends) on a further mortgage. I hope now Mr G. is married he will be steady and able to take his place again by the help of his wife's friends, as I think it would be their best way to do.

If I should be obliged to part with my interest in the places you so ably and satisfactorily fill, may I ask if you would purchase it and what is the most you would give considering all circumstances or wither it would not be agreeable for you to have them.

If it should be the case that I must part with it consequence of my loss at Huntingdon the Bank, which doubtless you have heard of the same, should the same be almost lost, which is near 800 pounds, I then must make the offer to some person and do think you are the most proper person to have it.

Your answer to these foregoing questions and observations will much oblige, dear sir, your humble servant.

My respectfull compliments to Mrs Fardell and family.

N.B.   Any other question you wish to ask about the Insurance will be answered.

Endorsement: Mr Abbott, 6 Jan. 1804, with answer.

[1] He married Mary Hatley, spinster, of St Neots. On 30th December, 1803, he sought licence to be married in the parish church of Eynesbury. In the marriage bond he is described as attorney-at-law, of the parish of Eynesbury (Huntingdon-shire County Record Office, Archdeaconry of Huntingdon: marriage allegations and bonds, G. 1785-1814).

20.   *John Fardell to William Abbott*

Lincoln, 27 January 1804.

In compliance with your request, I send you inclosed a bill for fifty pounds which I doubt not will meet with due honor, although I am too early in drawing upon them. You will send me your receipt for it, as for fees on account of Mr Green's office arising since Michaelmas last.

E

As Mr Green has executed another assignment to you, I think it may be proper and right for him to signify to me by letter in his own hand "that he has made an assignment of the whole of the fees of his office of Register under the Commissaries of Lincoln and Stow to Mr William Abbott, and that he authorizes and empowers me to pay the same to him, and that Mr Abbott's receipt for the fees of his office shall be my full discharge".
Mr Abbot, Upholder,
St Neots.

21. *William Abbott to John Fardell*

St Neots, 3 March 1804.

I beleive Mr Green has at last sold his places that are assigned to me—to whom I cannot tell, but I am ordered to go to Maule and Sweeting's office to make over the assignment with him next Friday, on which day I am to give up the profits and the purchaser to take possession of the same, I suppose. I write this to inform you to have the goodness to do as much buisness by that day as you can, or to inform me if the ye[ar] can be divided or not, or wither it would be right to take the average of the years or for me to decline and the purchaser to commence on the day the assignment is made. What he has made of it I cannott tell or who is the real purchaser, unless it is Mr Sweeting himself.[1]

You will also have the goodness to let me know by return of post what I am in your debt or if I may expect any thing more due on that [d]ay.

I will be much obliged to you for your kind advice in this matter, as I am quite a stranger in such things and am, dear sir, your humble servant.

Pray remember me to Mrs F., son, and all your kind family. Be so kind to give me the nissary information as soon as possible.

[1] On 17th March 1804 Hodgson wrote to Fardell: 'Rust and Sweeting have bought Sam: Green's Patent' (Cor. R. 5/18).

21a. *Draft of Fardell's reply endorsed*

I cannot give you any account of what the profits of the half year from Michaelmas day to Lady day next will amount to 'till I receive the returns from the different Surrogates which cannot be 'till after the Visitation in May. The best way will probably be for you and the purchaser to divide the year in proportion to the time. I cannot tell whether you will have any thing more to receive or not. There has been a good deal of [bus]iness done and it is probable there may be something more due, but it is impossible for me to tell 'till I know what licences have been dispatched, and get the returns from the Surrogates.

22. *John Fardell to Samuel Watkins Green*

Lincoln, 24 March 1804.

I find by your letter of the 8th inst. that you and Mr Abbott have assigned over *the whole of your interest* in the patents to Mr Rust and Mr Sweeting, and I am desired to pay the profits of the current half year into their hands.

I shall be glad to be informed whether you have made an absolute assignment to Messrs Rust and Sweeting, or whether you have reserved a power of redeeming the patents upon repayment of the sum they have advanced—also whether you have made any stipulation with Mr Abbott or the present assignees for the payment of the twenty-three pounds you have lately received from me.

23. *Samuel Watkins Green to John Fardell*

1 April 1804.

Your letter I should have answered sooner but have been prevented. (As you request) an assignment totally and without power of redemption I have been compelled to make. Since which I have understood there is in existence an Act by the Legislature to prevent things of that [*sic*]. If so, I feel it a duty incumbent up[on] me to inform the assignees thereof, and if you can be kind enough to favor me with a short abstract of the clause relative to the above, I shall thank you. Mr Abbott retained £20, supposing himself to be accountable to you, and the remaining £3 I had forgotten at the time but will take care to have you paid. You will be pleased to observe that you pay into Mr Abbott's hands no more than the average sum of £100 he will be intitled at the time of the assignment to Messrs Sweeting and Rust, so that the overplus may remain in your hands for my use up to the date of the assignment. Be so good as to let me hear from you as early as possible, and if you have drawn out your account be kind enough to let me know what is due to Mr Abbott and what to me. I leave home on Sunday next for a month. I trust I may hear from you before that time. I am dear sir, your truly and respectful ser[vant].

Endorsement: Mr Green, 1st April 1804, with answer thereto, acknowledging that an absolute assignment of his office was made to Messrs Rust and Sweeting, in answer to my letter of 24 March.

Post mark: St Neot's.

24. *John Fardell to Samuel Watkins Green*

Lincoln, 3 April 1804.

As you have made an absolute assignment of your offices totally and without power of redemption, you can have nothing farther to do with them, and your letter of the 7th of last month, signed by yourself and Mr Abbott, informing me of such assignment directs the future payments to be made to Messrs Rust and Sweeting.

I must therefore account to them. I presume the gentlemen to whom you have assigned the offices have taken care that the assignment is legal and valid, but if there should be any defect in it you will certainly be obliged to rectify it, or repay the money you have received. There was an Act of Parliament passed in the 5th year of King Edward VI, cap. 16, intitled an Act against buying and selling of offices, but whether it applies to such a case as yours, I cannot take upon myself to say.[1] I must beg that you will speak to Mr Abbott about the £23 due from you to me, and that he or you will point out how it is to [be] repaid to me. I am, dear sir, your obedient servant.

[1] 5 and 6 Edw. VI c. 16, an Act against buying and selling of offices. Anyone selling any office or deputation of any office relating to the administration of justice was to lose it and the bargain to be void. In 8 Jas. I it was resolved that offices in ecclesiastical courts were within this statute (E. Gibson, *Codex Iuris Ecclesiastici*, 2nd ed. 1761, p. 980).

25. *John Fardell to Lieutenant S. W. Green*, 21st Regiment of Foot, Ayr Barracks, Scotland.

Lincoln, 4 February 1804 [*recte* 1805].

I am sorry there should be any misunderstanding between you and Mr Abbott. It is impossible for me to form any judgment of the case between you unless I had the several agreements and deeds before me, but if you have made an absolute assignment of your office (which by your letter of the 1st of April last to me you say you have done), I see no probable means of your setting it aside. If you could raise the money to pay what Messrs Rust and Sweeting have advanced, perhaps they would reassign it to you, but I apprehend it is optional in them to do it or not, and that having assigned over the whole of your interest in the office you can have no legal redress.

I paid Mr Abbott thirty pounds in October 1803, £18 14s. 0d. on the 9th of November 1803, being the balance of the account to Michaelmas 1803, and in January 1804 I paid him fifty pounds more upon account. The balance of the account at Lady day 1804 I paid to Messrs Rust and Sweeting according to the joint order and direction of yourself and Mr Abbott.

On the 5th of January 1804 I sent you £20 and £3 you had when at Lincoln the 3rd of February[1]. You promised to remit both sums to me, and if Mr Abbott will not allow them, I must expect the repayment from you, according to your engagement. I am, dear sir, your very obedient servant.

[1] Fardell's accounts as deputy show that on 9th November 1803 William Abbott examined the account and the balance of £18 14s. 0d. due for the half year was paid to him as assignee and lawful attorney of Samuel Watkins Green. For the half year

from 29th September 1803 to 25th March 1804, £50 was paid to Mr. Abbott on account on 28th January, £23 advanced to Mr. Green, and the remaining £12 18s. 1d. was remitted to Messrs Rust and Sweeting, solicitors at Huntingdon, assignees of Mr. Green, on 24th July 1804. From this date until February 1808 it is stated that the proceeds were remitted to Messrs Rust and Sweeting at Huntingdon half yearly. In 1808 and 1809 they were paid to James Rust at Huntingdon, and from 29th September 1809 until March 1813, when this account ends, it is not stated to whom the proceeds were paid (R./Ac. 3/6).

INDEX
OF PERSONS, PLACES, AND SUBJECTS

J. W.
RUDDOCK
& SONS LTD
PRINTERS
LINCOLN